THE MASTER MUSICIANS

BRUCKNER

Derek Watson

OXFORD UNIVERSITY PRESS
1996

Oxford University Press, Great Clarendon Street, Oxford OX2 6DP

Oxford New York
Athens Auckland Bangkok Bogota Bombay
Buenos Aires Calcutta Cape Town Dar es Salaam
Delhi Florence Hong Kong Istanbul Karachi
Kuala Lumpur Madras Madrid Melbourne
Mexico City Nairobi Paris Singapore
Taipei Tokyo Toronto
and associated companies in
Berlin Ibadan

Oxford is a trade mark of Oxford University Press

First published 1975 by J.M. Dent & Sons Ltd
© Derek Watson 1975, 1996
Reprinted 1977
First paperback edition 1977
Second edition published by Oxford University Press 1996

British Library Cataloguing in Publication Data
Data available

Library of Congress Cataloging in Publication Data
Watson, Derek.
Bruckner / Derek Watson.
p. cm.—(Master musicians series)
Includes bibliographical references and index.
1. Bruckner, Anton, 1824–1896. 2. Composers—Austria—Biography.
I. Title. II. Series.
ML410.B88W26 1996 780'.92—dc20 [B] 96–35599
ISBN 0-19-816617-6

1 3 5 7 9 10 8 6 4 2

Typeset by Hope Services (Abingdon) Ltd
Printed in Great Britain
on acid-free paper by
Butler & Tanner Ltd
Frome and London

To Eileen

Preface to the first edition

There is no parallel to Bruckner among creative artists. Perhaps a fellow symphonist, Shostakovich, has an affinity in so far as he is also an out-wardly shy and unheroic personality who none the less speaks heroically in his scores. Bruckner's contemporaries failed miserably in their attempt to comprehend him—neither their erroneous conception of his music as symphonic Wagnerianism nor their pitting of his talents against those of the symphonist Brahms helps us even slightly towards an understanding of his genius. The enigma of Bruckner's personality, coupled with the 'difficulty' of his idiom, long beclouded attempts at serious interest in him outside Austria and Germany. In 1938 Sir Henry J. Wood wrote: 'On October 15 [1903] I produced Bruckner's seventh symphony. This was its first and last performance at the Promenades. The public would not have it then; neither will they now.' Two decades later this situation was quite reversed, and my distinguished predecessor in this series, Hans F. Redlich, wrote in the preface to the 1963 edition of *Bruckner and Mahler* of the marked increase of interest in both composers through-out the Western Hemisphere.

As I write a decade later still, and on the eve of the 150th anniversary of Bruckner's birth, it is gratifying to find almost every significant work of his available on disc, including a number of his early works and his smallest motets, many of them appearing on several labels. And, *pace* Sir Henry, that most enterprising and innovatory of English conductors, I have heard the very symphony that was disdained by the public of his day receive more than one ovation at the Promenades. 'Patience et longueur de temps/Font plus que force ni que rage', says La Fontaine's couplet. Patience was Bruckner's greatest virtue in his slow, monumen-tal unfolding. Passage of time has justified his patience. Like every other artist, Bruckner will no doubt continue to have his detractors. To those who are on the threshold of his music for the first time there is one word of encouragement and advice—patience.

Every biographer of Bruckner is indebted to the diligent researches of August Göllerich and Max Auer, to whom I add my own tribute and acknowledgement. I should like to express my thanks to all those who have lent encouragement, helpful advice and practical assistance to the preparation of this book, especially Mr Deryck Cooke, Dr Robert Simpson, Miss Eileen Skinner and Mr Ronald Stevenson.

My gratitude also to Mrs Joan James who typed my manuscript; to my parents who helped me see it through the press; and to Argo Records, C.B.S. Records, Music for Pleasure Ltd and Oryx Recordings Ltd for their assistance. Music examples appear by kind permission of Breitkopf & Härtel, London, on behalf of the copyright owners.

Edinburgh, 1974   D.W.

Preface to the second edition

When first writing about Bruckner in the early 1970s I could muster only half-a-dozen recordings of the Seventh Symphony on LP discs. The Gramophone Catalogue for 1996 lists no fewer than forty-four recordings on compact discs of this symphony. The virtue of patience referred to in the preface to the earlier edition of this book thus brings its rewards, and not only in recorded sounds, for there have been important new editions of the scores in the last twenty or so years. If anything, this has made the 'Bruckner problem' more complex, a fact that a new generation of scholars has not been slow to recognize. Seasoned observers of the composer's fortunes have made significant re-evaluations, too, notably Robert Simpson (to whom I am so indebted for his encouragement of my early work on Bruckner) in the 1992 revision of his authoritative study *The Essence of Bruckner*, particularly with regard to the Third Symphony and the String Quintet.

The most essential of recent Bruckner literature has been included in an expanded Appendix D to this book. I have amended and enlarged both the Calendar and Personalia sections, added WAB numbers to the Catalogue of Works, following the *Werkverzeichnis Anton Bruckner* of Renate Grasberger (Vienna, 1977), and have re-arranged the order of works in Appendix B to tally more exactly with recent volumes of the *Bruckner Gesamtausgabe* (BRGA).

Corrections to and expansions of my main text are mostly confined to discussion of critical reception, editions, and the works themselves in Chapters 8 to 15. Apart from weeding out some errors and planting a few new factual details, the biographical section is largely unchanged. By the standards of a mid-to-late nineteenth century artist Bruckner's life was relatively uneventful, and I have again resisted any urge to psycho-analyse, tempting though this might be in the case of such evidence of obsessions, frustrations, late development, social awkwardness, religious fervour, and—surprisingly, emphatically, and all-importantly—gigantic optimism and originality.

His originality was undeniable, even to his detractors. His optimism has been called into question given, say, the dark ending of the first movement of Symphony No. 8 in its revised form or the anguish of the climax of his last complete movement, the Adagio of No. 9. Certain also, surely, is the fact that his music is never resigned to defeat or despair, and although it contains the deepest tragedy and most searing revelations of spiritual pain, it is charged with such intensity that, for me, it is never negative or plagued by uncertainty. Yet these are mere words and Bruckner (save when setting sacred texts) was not good with words, and so we should be wary in applying them to his abstract creations.

Lack of optimism seen in his feverish rewritings of earlier scores is an entirely different matter. It was brought about by despondency following well intentioned but unhelpful criticism from those who misunderstood him. This in no way diminishes the affirmative originality seen, step by step, or wave by mighty wave, in his approach to each new movement: twenty-seven colossal symphonic strides, so to speak (and placing revisions aside), in the mature last seven of his eleven symphonies. The internal motion contained in these individual 'steps' may be helpfully if simplistically understood as a wave-like progression. (One of the accounts which first excited my interest in Bruckner was Tovey's description of the first movement to No. 6, with the development of the first main theme 'passing from key to key beneath a tumultuous surface, sparkling like the Homeric seas'.)

Sheer novelty was not his goal nor his great achievement. The essence of his struggle lay rather in his unceasing progress itself. Progress towards what? Illumination, peace ('a patient search for pacification' in Simpson's memorable phrase), a reconciliation of opposites, an attempt at finding the harmony and golden measure of the grand design. Furtwängler said that 'for all its excitement (which can be carried to the limits of human understanding) every masterpiece of tonal music radiates a profound, unshakeable, penetrating peace'. Beyond citing this 'tranquillity in the midst of motion' as a pronounced characteristic of Bruckner's art I make no attempt to foist further philosophy on his music, which he would have voiced only in terms of humility and the purest faith. What matters finally, even if he made no *final* statement of his goal in words or music, is that his works speak ever more resoundingly to us a century after his death.

I am grateful to Bruce Phillips for commissioning this revision to coincide with the centenary of the composer's death and at a time when no other monograph on Bruckner remained in print in English. To Julia Kellerman my thanks, too, for leading me once again so ably along editorial paths. I am deeply indebted to Will Scott for all sorts of patient help and advice, and to Tom Service and Erik Levi for stimulating ideas.

D.W.
West Linton, 1996

Contents

Illustrations

Childhood in Upper Austria

Austria in the decades leading up to the revolution of 1848, that is during the period known as the *Vormärz*, was a living example of feudalism. The various arms of the state wielded complete control and the official language with its stiff, formal, stereotyped phrases was characteristic of a period of deepest reaction and intolerance. Metternich's reactionary empire contained groups of the most primitive people in European society, and the Catholic peasantry were quite unaffected by the growing liberalism and sophistication of life that was occurring elsewhere in Europe. The iron grip of the State was reinforced by the authority of the Roman Catholic Church, which held the unswerving devotion of the peasantry.

Born during the reign of the Emperor Francis I (1768–1835) Joseph Anton Bruckner was a child of the *Vormärz*, and the environment and educational system of those years stamped his character for life. His birthplace, Ansfelden, is near Linz in the Traun district of Upper Austria. The river Danube flows through Upper Austria from the Bavarian city of Passau in the west and passes by Linz, the capital of the region, which was over two hours' journey from Ansfelden. The countryside around Ansfelden, bordered by the rivers Traun and Enns, presents a rich landscape of streams, valleys, meadows, and woods and contains two medieval cathedral towns, Enns and Steyr, and shelters resplendent monasteries. Within view of the Salzburg Alps in the west, this fertile area was exclusively peasant farming land.

The innumerable amusing anecdotes about the oddities of Bruckner's character can be explained, if not disposed of, by a few moments' reflection on these social and geographical factors of which he was a product. In an era when agnosticism gripped the thoughts of intellectuals and artists throughout Europe, he remained an unquestioning believer. Towards the end of a century that had begun with Beethoven scorning his patrons, Bruckner always remained humble in attitude to his superiors. In fashionable Vienna, where he spent almost the last thirty years of his life, he raised eyebrows and added spice to the pages of generations of biographers by retaining his Upper Austrian habits of dress, speech, and cautious manner. Countless quaint characteristics persisted that had their origins in his formative years prior to 1848, and the most important result of them was that as an artist he also stood outside the accepted boundaries of nineteenth-century romanticism. These characteristics have been so often repeated and so much exaggerated that there has arisen the case for Anton Bruckner, the country bumpkin. The rest of this book proposes to demolish that case.

Research has shown that the Bruckner family had lived in the vicinity of Linz for over four centuries before Anton's birth. Jörg Pruckner, a feudal peasant born around 1400, had a holding near Oed (twenty-five miles east of Linz) called the *Pruckhof*, and the family name derives from their living near a bridge—*Brücke*, or, in old Austrian, *Pruck*. Josef Bruckner, born in Pyhra near Oed in 1715, acquired some wealth by marriage and in leaving the family home turned from a long line of peasants and farmers who had prospered for a time, had owned quarries, had even in a few cases become aldermen and acquired nobility, and established himself in Oed as a house-owner, innkeeper, and broom-maker. One of his sons, another Joseph (1749–1831), followed in the trade of broom-making but married a school-master's daughter, Franziska Kletzer, and finally took up teaching and was posted to Ansfelden in 1776. The tenth of his twelve children, Anton, born in 1791, became his father's assistant and, in 1823, his successor. In the same year he married Theresia Helm (born 1801), the daughter of Ferdinand Helm, a civil servant and innkeeper from Neuzeug near Steyr. Of their eleven children, five survived infancy.

Thus their eldest son, Tonerl (the diminutive form of Anton in Upper Austrian dialect), born on 4 September 1824, was, like Schubert, a school-master's son. The position of school-master was the most respected one in the village next to that of priest, but in reality it meant a hard life with many extra duties and a miserable salary. One of the extra duties was to act as church organist and, so it seems, Tonerl's favourite place in church was next to his father on the organ bench. His mother, who had a fine singing voice and sang in the church choir, took the boy with her to High Mass from earliest childhood. At the church was an 'orchestra' of two violins, one double bass, clarinet, and horn, except on special occasions when two trumpeters and a timpanist were brought from Linz. The music of the day stemmed from the graduals and offertories for the liturgical year written by Michael Haydn for the Archbishop Hieronymus of Salzburg, which were taken by other composers as models to be followed. By the age of four Tonerl was playing a few hymns on the violin and not long after trying his father's spinet. The elder Bruckner was an enthusiastic musician, a member of the Linz Music Association, and did everything to stimulate the talent that began to appear in his son—the only one of his first four children to survive.

At ten the boy was able to deputize for his father at the organ, and by that time he had come to know what was to remain his lifelong spiritual home, the Augustinian monastery of St Florian. The journey to Linz being too long, visits to St Florian with its magnificent organ and opulent baroque architecture were frequent for the family.

By the spring of 1835 Tonerl had two younger sisters, Rosalia who was six, Josefa who was five, and a baby brother, Ignaz (1833–1913).[1] The eldest child was therefore sent from the crowded little house to live with his godfather and cousin Johann Baptist Weiss, school-teacher and organist at Hörsching. Weiss was a genuine artistic personality and the composer of a number of sacred works, including a Requiem in E flat major[2] which shows an individual and strongly devotional spirit. In his later years Bruckner expressed his lasting spiritual indebtedness to this man who gave him his first serious tuition in harmony, figured bass, and organ playing. This beneficial period which lasted until December 1836 also introduced him to a wider repertory of church music, including Mozart's Masses and Haydn's *The Creation, The Seven Last Words from the Cross*, and *The Seasons.* His general education was improved and there were his first attempts at composition. A short a cappella setting of Thomas Aquinas' Corpus Christi hymn 'Pange lingua' is his earliest extant choral work. This C major exercise in homophony spans Bruckner's entire creative career as he revised it as late as 1891. A work for chorus and instruments referred to by Bruckner on 14 July 1835 is now lost. Four organ preludes display daring if not academically sound harmonic imagination.

The close of 1836 saw Tonerl's father seriously ill and brought the twelve-year-old boy back to Ansfelden, where he took over some of his father's duties. These had proved a great strain for the older man's health—which is not surprising as his tasks as sexton included ringing church bells at four or five in the morning, and he often worked well into the night playing the fiddle at village dances to augment his meagre income. Tonerl saw his father die of consumption on 7 June 1837, and that very day his mother took him to St Florian to ask the prior, Michael Arneth, to accept him as a chorister. Arneth[3], who was interested in music and who often entertained the brothers Anton and Franz von Spaun, intimate friends of Schubert, admitted the boy and from that time on was his staunch supporter and friend. Bruckner's mother moved to Ebelsberg with her four children.

St Florian, ten miles from Linz, is an ancient monastery which dates in its present form from 1686 to 1751. The architect was Carlo Carlone and the building was completed under the supervision of Jakob Prandtauer and Jacob Steinhuber. Nestling in the terraces of the Upper

[1] One more child born to his parents was to survive: Maria Anna ('Nani', 1836–70) became Bruckner's favourite sister and was for five years to be his housekeeper. Josefa died in 1874; Rosalia in 1898.

[2] Published by Ernst Lanninger, 1892.

[3] Born 1771; prior of St Florian, 1823–54.

Austrian hills, it is one of Austria's finest examples of Baroque architecture, and not only was it to shelter Bruckner in his days as a scholar
but also throughout his career remained his retreat from the world, and
represents much of what characterizes Bruckner the man and artist.
Baroque splendour, the high towers, the hundreds of windows, the
elegant marble, the paintings, the treasures of the library and, above
all, the *Stiftkirche* itself with its three organs made a profound impression on the boy which should not be underrated. The great organ (now
known as the 'Bruckner Organ') was built by Chrismann in 1771 and
had at least seventy-four stops. Tonerl's education continued with
lessons in reading, writing, and arithmetic and included organ and
piano lessons from the noted organist Anton Kattinger, violin lessons
from Franz Gruber (a pupil of Beethoven's friend Schuppanzigh) and
studies in musical theory. Figured-bass lessons were given by the headmaster, Michael Bogner, in whose home Tonerl lodged with two other
choirboys. When he was fourteen official schooling ended and more
time was spent at the organ, particularly at the practice of improvisation. A year later Tonerl's voice broke and although replaced in the
choir, he continued to take an active part for a while in music-
making at St Florian, both as violinist and as deputy organist for certain minor services.

The time came for deciding on a career. Bruckner seems to have been
guided by the axiom 'like father, like son' and accordingly he was prepared for the *Präparandie* (teacher-training school) in Linz, and passed
the entrance examination on 1 October 1840. Already he seems to have
considered financial prospects and the welfare of his mother and family
carefully and conscientiously, and this may have had some bearing on
his choice of profession.

The ten-month course in Linz included plenty of musical studies as
custom ordained that village schoolmasters were to be responsible for
music in the church. His teacher was Johann August Dürrnberger,
author of a book on musical theory to which Bruckner later said he
owed all, and which he used as the basis of his own teaching in his
Vienna years. The activity of the provincial capital (population then
c. 20,000) must have been a sharp contrast to the quietness of his boy-
hood villages and the seclusion of St Florian. Musical horizons, too,
were widened. Dürrnberger introduced him to Bach's *Die Kunst der Fuge*
and the fugues of Albrechtsberger. While the worldly pleasures of the
theatre were denied to students of the *Präparandie*, Bruckner absorbed
more and more Viennese classical church music, especially the works of
Joseph and Michael Haydn and those of minor local figures such as
Zenetti, Johann Keinersdorfer, and Johann Baptist Schiedermayer. The
repertory at St Florian included Albrechtsberger, Aumann, Eybler,
Aiblinger, Bühler, Caldara, and of course Gregorian chant. But secular
music found its place, too, and the secular concerts at St Florian together

with the meetings of the Linz Music Association had already brought to his attention overtures and small works by Rossini, Beethoven, Weber, and Mendelssohn, together with a few symphonies by Mozart and Beethoven.

Bruckner was a model student, scoring 'gut' or 'sehr gut' in every subject for his final examination in Linz which qualified him as 'assistant teacher for elementary schools'—a fine achievement, as most students took two attempts at the course before gaining a certificate. He then spent a few weeks at St Florian, possibly also visiting his family at Ebelsberg, and his official student days were over.

Years of apprenticeship

In October 1841 Bruckner was appointed assistant teacher in Windhaag, a small village of about thirty-five houses by the Bohemian border and near Freystadt. On the whole this was a time of servile drudgery for the young assistant, who found himself bound to a hard master, the teacher Franz Fuchs[1], overloaded with menial tasks and subject to many humiliations. He consequently regarded Windhaag with much the same feelings that Mozart had held for Salzburg. Life followed the pattern of his father's beginning each day by tolling the morning bell at five (4 a.m. in summer!) and frequently playing the violin at village dances to augment his wage of twelve florins per annum. Out of this paltry sum the seventeen-year-old boy, already remarkably cautious, paid his first contribution to an insurance policy for his old age. He turned for consolation to the things that he was always to revere—his religion, the church organ, and his composition, completing a short Mass in C major for solo contralto, accompanied by the poor forces he had available: organ and two horns. The alto solo was written for Anna Jobst who had the loveliest voice in the choir. He continued his studies of *Die Kunst der Fuge* and the fugues of Albrechtsberger and found a friendly, musical family, that of the weaver Sücka, with whom he formed a band in which he played second fiddle at country inns for wedding entertainments and other celebrations.

When Arneth came to Windhaag on a tour of inspection, Fuchs took the opportunity to express his extreme dissatisfaction with Bruckner, who had particularly irked him by failing to do manual duties in the fields such as shifting manure, and who had further upset him by showing such keen musical ambitions. Arneth reacted in effect with a kind of promotion rather than a punishment and Bruckner found himself transferred to Kronstorf on 23 January 1843. A much happier time ensued in the house of his superior, Franz S. Lehofer, and his wife, and Bruckner always remembered them with affection. The village, situated between Enns and Steyr, was half the size of Windhaag and just within walking distance of St Florian, to which Bruckner was a frequent visitor. Soon

---

[1] Fuchs (1788–1860) was Windhaag's school-master from 1822 till his death.

his salary was raised to twenty florins. His Kronstorf days involved much music-making with new friends and he sang in a male-voice choir. Through the kindness of a farmer, Josef Födermeyer, he had placed in his classroom an old spinet on which he practised Bach.

In Enns Bruckner renewed his acquaintance with the fine organist and choirmaster Leopold Edler von Zenetti, whom he had known at St Florian, and took lessons from him in musical theory three times a week. Zenetti's teaching was based on the textbook of Daniel Gottlob Türk and J. S. Bach's chorales and *The Well-tempered Clavier*. Bruckner also made good friends with the priest in Steyr and this gave him the opportunity of practising on the fine Chrismann organ there. Steyr was to be another spiritual retreat for him in his later years, and so to the influence of baroque architecture was added that of the Renaissance and Gothic ages for which Steyr is noted, in particular the great German Gothic *Stadtpfarrkirche*. Also in Steyr he met Karoline Eberstaller, the daughter of a French general. She had played duets with Schubert whenever he stayed in Steyr in the last years of his life, and now she introduced Bruckner to his piano duets which they played together.

Composition developed during the Kronstorf years including two secular works, a fairly ambitious chamber cantata, *Vergissmeinnicht* (1845) and a male-voice a cappella setting of words by the parish priest of Kronstorf, *An dem Feste* (1843); both were later revised by Bruckner, the latter as late as 1893 when it was renamed *Tafellied*. The sacred choral works of this period are much influenced by classical models and show that he had securely grasped the principles of composition, but so far without any clear individuality. They include several settings of the Mass, a 'Libera me', two settings of 'Tantum ergo', and three 'Asperges me'. Apart from additional musical studies, organ practice, music-making, composition, and his heavy rota of official duties, he was occupied in preparing for an examination (the *Konkursprüfung*) which every assistant teacher had to pass four years after his initial qualification. He achieved this with marked success on 29 May 1845 and even surprised his old teacher Dürrnberger by the quality of his contrapuntal improvisation at the organ. He was now a fully equipped school-teacher.

St Florian had a vacancy for an assistant teacher, and Bruckner found himself back there in that capacity on 25 September with a salary of thirty-six florins per annum and filling the role of deputy organist to his former teacher Kattinger. For a decade he taught the lowest two classes in the school, and music was of necessity a leisure-time activity throughout this period. Nevertheless he maintained his organ practice for two hours each day under Kattinger's supervision, concentrating on improvisation and the works of Bach, and he frequently travelled to hear recitals in Linz. He now worked through Marpurg's *Treatise on the Fugue* in a new edition by Simon Sechter. Compositions of this time were largely for chorus and included a Requiem of March 1845 (now

7

lost) for his friend Johann Nepomuk Deschl, school-master at Kirchberg. The organ music which has survived is unimportant, and probably none of his works at this time reflects his growing skill at improvisation. The male-voice choruses he wrote were the result of his singing first bass in a newly formed male quartet. The second bass was the gardener at St Florian, Johann Nepomuk Hueber, who was to marry Bruckner's sister Rosalia and later settle with her in Vöcklabruck. In 1847 Bruckner was deeply impressed on hearing Mendelssohn's *St Paul* in Linz, and the influence of Mendelssohn on his work became marked.

Throughout his teaching days at St Florian he stayed again in the house of the headmaster Bogner, and was much attracted to the daughter of the house, Aloisia; but the romance came to nothing, leaving its mark only in a few songs and piano pieces of these years such as *Frühlingslied* and the *Lancier-Quadrille* for piano. (The latter is a curiosity that must rank as Bruckner's nearest approach to operatic fantasy: the first two and the last of its four movements quote themes from *Der Wildschütz* and *Zar und Zimmermann* respectively, works by Lortzing that had recently been performed at the Linz opera house.) Another set of quaint *Quadrille* for piano duo were intended for the daughter of the *Stiftsrichter* at St Florian, and Bruckner's pupil, Marie Ruckensteiner. In all these there is surely an echo of Bruckner's dance-hall experiences.[2]

The godfather of Bruckner's brother Ignaz, Franz Seiler, a judicial actuary, bought a Bösendorfer grand piano, and Bruckner had access to this fine instrument. In 1848 Seiler had a sudden heart attack and died, and this had two important results. The first was that Bruckner inherited the Bösendorfer piano, which he used throughout his life, and the second was the beginning of a work in grateful memory of his benefactor, the Requiem in D minor, completed in 1849 and first performed at St Florian on 13 September of that year—a landmark in his creative career and his first truly notable large work. A second performance of the deeply-felt Requiem took place in Kremsmünster on 11 December.

The year of revolutions, 1848, affected Bruckner and St Florian mildly. Bruckner enrolled in the National Guard and took part in some military exercises. More important, in March Kattinger was transferred to Kremsmünster and Bruckner became provisional organist—his first step towards a professional musical career. On his departure Kattinger had provided Arneth with an assessment of Bruckner's skills that amounted to a paean of praise, and in July 1848 the 'provisional organist' acquired another glowing testimonial as to his fine musicianship and abilities as composer and player from the then renowned organist and composer Josef Pfeiffer of Seitenstetten in Lower Austria.

[2] Another set of Three Little Pieces for piano four-hands (1853–5) are for children (tne offspring of his friend the lawyer Josef Marböck) and contain Bruckner's teaching fingerings. The last piece bears a tempo marking later to become very characteristic: 'langsam, feierlich'.

Fig. 1 St Florian

Promotion, however, seems to have disquieted Bruckner and awakened indecisiveness: dissatisfaction with his teaching life and a growing longing for a musical profession, conflicting with his dependence on a financially secure position. It was the beginning of a spell of unhappiness and fretfulness that overshadowed his remaining years at St Florian. He even applied for the position of a clerk in the civil service for which he claimed to feel a vocation, pointing out that he had been studying Latin and physics; but to the great benefit of musical history this particular application was unsuccessful, although he did work as a voluntary clerk at the local Court and acquired some legal knowledge. He also added a testimonial for Latin studies to his growing collection of certificates. Karl Seiberl, a friend with whom Bruckner had shared lodgings when they had been fellow choirboys at St Florian a decade earlier, was at this time studying law at Vienna. Anton felt a little envy, not only for Karl's vocation-to-be, but also for his friend's university life with the attendant musical opportunities of the big city. The contrast with his own lot, that of an unmarried, lonely provincial schoolmaster, perhaps doomed to remain for ever in an environment that seemed less and less appreciative of his creative talents, must have been the wistful reflection of his sadder hours.

In 1850 Bruckner was shocked to learn of the fate of his godfather and former teacher, Weiss. Innocently Weiss had accepted the responsibility for a church fund from which, unknown to him, a large sum had been embezzled. On the morning of 10 July a police officer approached his cottage and the poor, terrified man fled to the graveyard and killed himself. Bruckner tried several times in vain to persuade the church authorities to entrust to him the skull of his revered relative, and it is a sign of the affection he felt for him that as late as 1895 the ailing composer wrote the last of many requests to the church authorities at Hörsching for a Mass to be said for the repose of Weiss's soul.

At this time Bruckner embarked upon a two-year course at the *Unter-Realschule* of Linz to improve his general education preparatory to becoming a high-school teacher. Although his salary as provisional organist rose to forty-four florins and he became entitled to free board and lodging, his unhappiness continued—an unsuccessful love-affair with a sixteen-year-old girl, Antonie Werner, and, about the same time, criticism from his colleagues for devoting too little energy to teaching and too much to music. This censure hurt the conscientious Bruckner and he was not placated until he had obtained a written testimonial from his superiors confirming his good conduct and reliable character, and a written guarantee from Arneth assuring his salary. The friends with whom he had enjoyed singing vocal quartets were now dispersed, married, or dead. He wrote, on 19 March 1852, to his successor-to-be as organist at St Florian, Josef Seiberl (brother of Karl): 'You see how everything has altered. I sit in my small room, all alone and in the deepest melancholy.'

Early in 1852 Bruckner paid his first visit to Vienna in order to see Ignaz Assmayer, court conductor, notable composer of sacred music, pupil of Michael Haydn, and friend of Schubert. To him he wrote on 30 July, complaining bitterly of his life at St Florian, of the indifference to music and musicians there, and of the lack of anyone to whom he could open his heart. He completed settings of Psalm 114 (dedicated to Assmayer) and Psalm 22, and of an impressive Magnificat in B flat major. Mendelssohn and the Viennese classics were still his principal models, and in an interesting letter of September 1853 his friend Scharschmidt (a lawyer in Linz) advised him to give up the idea of becoming a civil servant or of changing his job and continued: 'You are making a mistake if you look exclusively to Mendelssohn for your instruction. In any case you should take from the sources he did, that is Sebastian Bach, whom you should study thoroughly.'

On 24 March 1854 Michael Arneth, the prior of St Florian, died. After the Requiem Mass two works were sung that were specially written by the thirty-year-old composer, whose career he had aided so much: *By Arneth's Grave* and a 'Libera' in F minor. On 1 August his Magnificat was first heard at St Florian and a week later the Missa Solemnis in B flat minor was completed. This Mass, which is the most important milestone between the Requiem of 1849 and the great choral works of the 1860s, was first performed at the enthroning of Arneth's successor, Friedrich Theophil Mayr, on 14 September and aroused much enthusiasm. Bruckner was slighted by the fact that no one asked him to the banquet which followed the ceremony. The tale is told that he took himself off to a nearby inn, ordered a lonely but ample meal of five courses with three different wines, and began his private celebration with the words, '*That* Mass deserves it!' More achievements followed in the form of further certificates—one for passing an organ examination in Vienna on 9 October at which he improvised a double fugue before Assmayer, Sechter, and Preyer, and the other of January 1855 for passing his examination for the qualification of high-school teacher at Linz, with 'very good' in all subjects. Any veracity given to the many later caricatures of Bruckner as a 'country bumpkin' can thus be totally discredited.

Robert Führer, an organist from Prague, arrived in St Florian in 1855, and Bruckner showed him his Missa Solemnis and improvised on the organ. Führer gave him an excellent testimonial and advised him to take lessons in strict harmony and counterpoint with the Viennese teacher Simon Sechter. As Mayr (a keen music lover and son of a Kapellmeister) had given similar advice to him after hearing the Mass, Bruckner set off in July with the work and Führer's reference. Sechter immediately accepted the applicant as a pupil but advised him to leave St Florian—advice that made him more agitated than ever about his future. He began to look around for a post as musician and secretly and unsuccessfully applied for the post of organist at Olmütz (Olomouc) Cathedral; but this action brought him a sharp censure from the prior at St Florian.

Simon Sechter was born in 1788 in Friedberg, Bohemia, and lived in Vienna from 1804. In 1824 he became Voříšek's successor as court organist. In 1828 Schubert, only weeks before his death, approached him for counterpoint lessons, and in 1850 he was appointed a professor of composition at the Vienna Conservatory. His pupils included Thalberg and Vieuxtemps, and he was the composer of oratorios, Masses, operas (including a burlesque opera *Ali hitsch-hatsch*), organ music, and over 5,000 fugues. Sechter was a profound thinker and an energetic, diligent craftsman who wrote at least one fugue a day. His interests included numerology, as seen in his '104 Variations on a theme of 104 bars' (which is a tantalizingly curious pointer to Bruckner's later numeromania and might well indicate an affinity between the two men). Sechter was a naturally generous man and through his own kindness reduced himself to poverty in his last years. As a teacher he was the author of a three-volume treatise *Die Grundsätze der musikalischen Komposition* (The Principles of Musical Composition), 1853–5, based on a Rameau-inspired theory of 'inter-dominants'.[3] Bruckner thoroughly mastered Sechter's rigorous system, which was exclusively a study of the music of the past (figures such as Marpurg, Türk, Kirnberger, and of course Rameau), and it is possible that this found a practical outlet in the

---

[3] Jean Philippe Rameau (1683–1764) first set down the theory of the fundamental bass, the basic root of each chord and its inversions. A systematic progression by intervals of 4ths or 5ths of these roots, which need not be audible or sounded, governs the rules of modulation. For further details of Sechter's development of Rameau's and other harmonic theories see the note on Sechter in Appendix C.

harmonic clarity, advanced modulations, and striking tonal contrasts of his mature works.

But the strict discipline of the years with Sechter may have had a more significant result. All Bruckner's works prior to this time are competent, orthodox and in some cases highly effective, but they give little or no hint of the outburst of originality that shortly followed. Perhaps Bruckner laboured so hard at orthodox procedures while studying with Sechter (a period almost totally devoid of original compositions) that he worked them out of his system and cleared the way for new thoughts. Robert Simpson has written: 'It is possible that Sechter unknowingly brought about Bruckner's originality by insisting that it be suppressed until it could no longer be contained.'[4] In any sphere it is not uncommon for something to work itself to an extreme pitch, fall away exhausted, and give way to something new and fresh. It is the pattern of many steps in musical history and it suggests that Bruckner's years with Simon Sechter formed an important bridge to the awakening of his art—a bridge that no other composer had crossed in quite the same way.

[4] *The Essence of Bruckner* (London, 1967; rev. edn., 1992).

3

Linz

In November 1855 the post of cathedral organist in Linz became vacant and on the 13th of the month a preliminary examination of candidates took place. On that morning the organ-tuner arrived at St Florian and expressed surprise that Bruckner was not in Linz to apply for the position. He was reluctantly cajoled into going to Linz, where he called upon Dürrnberger. He was hesitant about taking the examination, fearing both the future and the opinion of his superiors at St Florian, but accompanied Dürrnberger to listen to the other applicants, both of whom, it transpired, failed to satisfy the examiners in providing a fugal improvisation on a set theme. Dürrnberger approached Bruckner, who was praying, and insisted: 'Tonerl, you *must* play!' Bruckner then sat at the organ and improvised with such skill and contrapuntal mastery that the result of the competition was obvious. On hearing that he had been successful, the prior of St Florian gave him his blessing for the new venture.

Still Bruckner hesitated. There was a final examination on 25 January 1856, before which written applications had to be submitted. Bruckner made no move, but was firmly persuaded and pressed into action. At the same time he was told to remember to dress carefully when meeting influential people and never to appear again 'in your overcoat which was even missing a button, and with a scarf around your neck'. These details sorted out, Bruckner faced three other candidates at the January audition and displayed 'such exceptional ability' that he was appointed. But his agonies of uncertainty were resolved only when he received an assurance that his job at St Florian would be kept open for him for two years in case he felt he wanted to come back. Thus Bruckner, now in his thirty-second year, cautiously embarked on his professional musical career.

Life in Linz was hectic. Bruckner was organist at both the cathedral and the *Pfarrkirche*, he took piano pupils, practised for hours each day at the organ, and became an active member (and shortly afterwards librarian) of the Linz choral society, the *Liedertafel 'Frohsinn'*. On the other hand, he was released from the monotonous round of teaching duties, had free lodgings (a flat with two rooms and kitchen) with a salary of about 450 florins (ten times his St Florian stipend), and he made many friends in the lively town, including Moritz von Mayfeld and his wife, and the brothers Alois and Rudolf Weinwurm. As later in the Vienna years, he became a well-known figure in local restaurants and cafés where he indulged his passion for regional specialities, or spent late evenings with young friends; he enjoyed the occasional cigar and his regular snuff. He eagerly attended dances and balls till late in life, and was a good dancer. Early in September 1856 Bruckner, with the *Liedertafel*, visited Salzburg for the centenary celebrations of Mozart's birth. While there he took part in a competition in organ improvisation at the cathedral, with Robert Führer as his rival.

The organ of the old cathedral in Linz, built by Chrismann and one of the finest of Austrian instruments, still exists as Bruckner knew it. A third manual was added during his years there, at his suggestion. Bruckner's favourite organ in the district was at the monastery of Wilhering—a small but delightful one-manual-and-pedals instrument which also still exists. He was again fortunate in his superior, Bishop Franz Josef Rudigier, a genuine lover of music, who became a warm friend and admirer and was perhaps the first person to appreciate and foster the early signs of his creative maturity.

Each day anything up to seven hours was devoted to exercises for Sechter, the tuition being largely carried on by correspondence. After receiving on one occasion *seventeen* notebooks filled with exercises in double counterpoint, Sechter wrote back:

> I really must implore you to take more care of yourself and to allow yourself sufficient relaxation. I can assure you that I am fully convinced of your thoroughness and eagerness and I do not want your health to suffer under too great a mental strain. I feel I have to tell you that I have never had a more dedicated pupil.[1]

Bruckner made the journey to Vienna twice a year, during Advent and Lent when the organ was silent in church. He became friendly with Sechter on these visits of six or seven weeks' duration, and spent every day from morning till evening in his teacher's home. At the end of each term he insisted on having a testimonial about his progress. When, on 10 July 1858, he sat an examination in harmony, figured bass, and organ-playing, Sechter wrote in his testimonial that 'Bruckner shows much versatility in improvisation and in developing a theme and may therefore be counted as one of the finest of organists'. A Viennese critic, Ludwig Speidel, attended Bruckner's organ-playing in the *Piaristenkirche* on this occasion, and wrote an article full of praise in the *Wiener Zeitung*. Step by step Bruckner completed the various stages of Sechter's course, passing elementary counterpoint on 12 August 1859, advanced counterpoint on 3 April 1860, and canon and fugue on 26 March 1861, thus concluding his theoretical studies and receiving a final glowing

[1] Letter of January 1860.

testimonial. Sechter was so completely satisfied that he celebrated the occasion by writing a fugue and dedicating it to Bruckner.

Meanwhile Bruckner's mother had died, on 11 November 1860. She had been alone in Ebelsberg for the past five years since the death of her blind sister-in-law with whom she had shared house. He was greatly upset by her death and regretted that she had never joined him in Linz as he had frequently urged.

In the same month Bruckner was appointed conductor of the *Liedertafel 'Frohsinn'*, which provided a welcome opportunity for more practical music-making after his years of theoretical study, and was also a new stimulus towards composition. After his final examination with Sechter, Bruckner was able to enjoy to the full his activities with the choir, and his first concert appearances as composer-conductor. His choir visited numerous choral festivals; their performances drew much praise and caught the attention of Johann Herbeck in Nürnberg. An influential musician, Herbeck was to become a firm friend of Bruckner's and a faithful promoter of his work in the Vienna years. A fine setting of 'Ave Maria' for seven-part chorus was first performed in Linz on 12 May, and the occasion was rightly seen by the *Linzer Zeitung* as a 'splendid demonstration' of Bruckner's powerful new compositional language following his long studies. While the choir was in Nürnberg during June, he fell for the charms of yet another young girl, called Olga, a waitress in restaurant frequented by the choir. One evening the choir decided to play a prank on Bruckner: they persuaded Olga, seductively dressed, to go up to a room where they had left Bruckner alone. Her entrance did not amuse him at all, and he ran from the restaurant, insulted, annoyed, and upset and at once resigned his conductorship of the choir.

Bruckner applied for the directorship of the *Dommusikverein und Mozarteum* in Salzburg, but as a result of various intrigues the post was awarded elsewhere. He then applied for the diploma of the Vienna Conservatory, a qualification which would entitle him to teach harmony and counterpoint in schools of music. In October he submitted Sechter's testimonials, some counterpoint exercises and a number of free compositions, and in November he was examined at the organ of the *Piaristenkirche*, Vienna, by representatives of the Austrian musical hierarchy: Herbeck, Hellmesberger, Sechter, Dessoff, and the schools' supervisor, Moritz Adolf Becker. It was his greatest examination triumph, and the effect of his improvisation on a long and difficult theme was summed up by Herbeck with the words: 'He should have examined us.' It was an occasion not unlike Walther before the Mastersingers, but Bruckner still had to face his Beckmesser, who was alive and well in Vienna, too. Meanwhile another success followed in December, when two of his works, the Psalm 146 for soloists, chorus, and orchestra, and the offertory 'Afferentur regi' for mixed chorus, three trombones, and organ, were first performed at Linz.

About this time he met Otto Kitzler, cellist and conductor at the municipal theatre in Linz. The meeting was perfectly timed, for Kitzler, although only in his twenties and a small figure when compared with the renowned Sechter, was able to share with Bruckner his keen interest in contemporary music and his knowledge of orchestration. Bruckner took lessons from the younger man in musical form and orchestration. His early work included analyses of Beethoven sonatas and of works by Mendelssohn and an orchestration of the first movement of Beethoven's *Pathétique* Sonata. Kitzler encouraged Bruckner to compose, and in 1862 some choral works (including a cantata for the laying of the foundation stone of the new Linz Cathedral on 1 May), a String Quartet in C minor, a march for military band, another for orchestra (in D minor), and three short orchestral pieces were composed, as well as a number of exercises in piano-sonata writing. These instrumental works were regarded by Bruckner as student exercises and nothing more.[2]

On 13 February 1863 Kitzler unknowingly performed his greatest service to his pupil. He mounted the first Linz performance of Wagner's *Tannhäuser*, and in their lessons he and Bruckner studied the score together, along with Liszt's symphonic poems. Within a year or two Bruckner was to be labelled (and to this day is often confusedly thought to be) a Wagnerian symphonist. This was to bring him a great deal of misery in later years, and was to hamper understanding of his music long after his death. Though the extent of Wagner's influence upon him will be discussed in a later chapter, it is essential to see his early Wagnerian experiences in perspective. Undoubtedly the works of Wagner which he heard in the 1860s had a tremendous effect on him, opening up new concepts of harmony, orchestration and time-scale. Yet he was thirty-eight and his musical foundations were already securely laid: the baroque composers whom he had sung at St Florian, mastered at the organ, and studied with Sechter; the German Gothic tradition; and the early romantics—Schubert, Weber, and Mendelssohn. Furthermore he was no mean contrapuntist, as is shown by accounts of his improvisation and by a work such as the Missa Solemnis of 1854, and no stranger to the skills of subtle harmonic effects: many pieces containing 'Wagnerian' harmony date from years before he was spellbound by turning the pages of the score of *Tannhäuser*. But Wagner was the fuse that set these foundations alight and awoke Bruckner's individuality.

In 1862 he applied without success for the post of *Expektant* organist (organist-designate) at the Imperial Court Chapel (the *Hofkapelle*). On Christmas Eve he began an Overture in G minor and completed it on 22 January. This, his first really impressive orchestral essay, was still

---

[2] A sketch book of 130 pages, formerly owned by Joseph Schalk, was discovered in 1949. Used between 1861 and 1863, it includes exercises, sketches, and compositions written for Kitzler. The only items from it that have been published are the String Quartet and a sonata movement in G minor for piano. The sketch book is in private ownership in Munich.

regarded by the composer as a mere study, as was his somewhat less effective Symphony in F minor, written in three months between February and May 1863. Around this time Kitzler gave performances of Wagner's *The Flying Dutchman* and *Lohengrin*, which Bruckner presumably attended. On 10 July Kitzler declared Bruckner to be a master, and Bruckner commented later that he felt like a watchdog that had at last snapped his chain. In the same year that Kitzler left Linz (he departed in September 1863) another champion of modern music arrived. Ignaz Dorn, violinist and composer, became second conductor at the opera. He introduced Bruckner to Liszt's *Faust Symphony* and enthused about Berlioz as well as Wagner. Two other works completed this year are important stages in Bruckner's unfolding: the Psalm 112, written in June and July, with which he felt he had mastered both choral and orchestral composition, and a large-scale work for male chorus and brass band, *Germanenzug*, which he regarded as his first real composition and which was his first work to be published (in 1865). In the summer he took a holiday, visiting the Salzkammergut.

Several scholars have held that the first version of a Symphony in D minor, now called 'die Nullte' or No. 0, was written in the period 1863–4. This attribution of date has become highly contentious and presents one of the few such chronological problems in Bruckner's output. Its origins are in the composer's remark made to his chosen biographer, August Göllerich, that he had written the work in Linz. Göllerich and Auer in their biography place the early D minor symphony in this period on the basis that between the completion of Psalm 112 and *Germanenzug*, in July and August of 1863, Bruckner wrote nothing of significance until we know him to have begun his Mass in D minor. The *Linzer Zeitung* reported him to be at work on the Mass on 4 June 1864. There are, however, several drawbacks to the theory of the symphony being composed during that winter. First, not a scrap of autograph material belonging to it has been found relating to 1863–4. Secondly, Bruckner's comment to Göllerich was made in 1895 when he was frequently confused about the exact dating of early works. At that time in 1895 he drew the symbol Ø on three pages of his manuscript of the D minor symphony dating from 1869. This gave rise to its subsequent name. Importantly though, Bruckner did not destroy the piece along with other works he deemed unworthy for posterity. Instead, as well as the clear blue pencil noughts, he merely sought to dissociate it from the official canon of his numbered symphonies by writing 'ungiltig . . . ganz nichtig . . . annulirt' (not valid . . . completely void . . . nullified) at various places in the manuscript. This manuscript of 1869 is dated section by section from 24 January, the start, until 12 September, the conclusion. Bruckner had by 1869 moved to Vienna but, significantly for this controversial point, he returned to Linz for the summer holidays and there, in August and early September, brought each of the four movements to their final form. Thus it could be said that the symphony was written (in the sense of all four movements being completed) in Linz in 1869. It may be added that for Göllerich and Auer the significance of the Ø meant, in Bruckner's code, composed before Symphony No. 1 (i.e. the C minor of 1865–6). On the other hand, Orel, Redlich, and other scholars[3] have forcefully denied that the 1869 D minor symphony has necessarily any forebear. For the moment we will rest this thorny problem only to grasp it anew when our account reaches 1869 and further discussion of 'die nullte Sinfonie'.

Returning to the autumn of 1863, in late September he spent a day or two at the eleventh Music Festival in Munich. While there he called on Franz Lachner, a leading conductor and former pupil of Sechter, who had been friendly with Schubert and admired by Beethoven. Lachner, who subsequently joined the anti-Wagner camp, showed interest in the F minor symphony. The only works definitely belonging to the next few months are trifles. An F sharp minor piano piece in the manner of Mendelssohn's *Songs Without Words* bears the date 19 October 1863: *Stille Betrachtung an einem Herbstabend* (Quiet Contemplation on an Autumn Evening). It was dedicated to one of his young piano students, Emma Thaner, who had taken weekly lessons with him for about six years and for whom he had formed a strong affection. Alas, these feelings were not reciprocated, nor did Emma learn her teacher's piece, which contains the idea of a lover waiting for a sweetheart who does not appear. 'Autumn sighing' is written on Bruckner's manuscript. Such unhappy attempts at love were to cast frequent shadows. Time and time again Bruckner fell hopelessly in love with girls in their late teens, and the result was always the same. He was liked as a character but was too old to be considered as a husband—he was now forty. Late in 1864 he wrote to Rudolf Weinwurm threatening to emigrate to Russia or Mexico. (Certain far-away, mysterious lands held a fascination for him—Mexico, Russia, or the North Pole).

In April he wrote another occasional piece, *Um Mitternacht*, for alto solo, male chorus, and piano. But the great leap forward creatively in 1864 was the Mass in D minor, his first truly individual large-scale work, written throughout the summer and complete by 29 September. This Mass was also his greatest public triumph to date as a composer. The first performance on 20 November at Linz was received with acclaim, and a concert performance followed in December. Bishop Rudigier admitted that he had been unable to pray during the performance owing to the beauty and artistry of the music. It was Bruckner's first important

---

[3] For important recent discussion of the chronology of the D minor symphony see Hawkshaw: 'The Date of Bruckner's "Nullified" Symphony in D Minor' (details in Appendix D) and Finscher, Ludwig: 'Zur Stellung der "Nullten" Sinfonie in Bruckners Werk' in Mahling: *Anton Bruckner: Studien zu Werk and Wirkung* (Tutzing, 1988), pp. 63–79.

work to be heard in Vienna, at the *Hofkapelle* under Herbeck on 10 February 1867.

In January 1865 he began a symphony in C minor which had advanced quite far by the spring, when he received an invitation from Wagner himself to attend the first performance of *Tristan und Isolde* in Munich in May. On arrival in Munich he found that the première had been postponed owing to the indisposition of Frau Schnorr (Isolde). So for two weeks he was in Wagner's presence: 'I introduced myself to the Master who proved unusually kind and friendly towards me, seeming to take a liking to me at once. I could not even bring myself to sit down in his presence at first, but he was reassuringly congenial and invited me to join his circle every evening.'

It is interesting to note that in studying *Tristan* Bruckner used a piano score without text—a sign of how unconcerned he was with opera as drama. He showed the beginnings of the C minor Symphony to Hans von Bülow, who at thirty-five was more approachable than he later became, and who was enthusiastic; Anton Rubinstein also found the work 'interesting and talented'. Bruckner was too afraid to show it to Wagner. He had to go back to Linz before the first night of *Tristan* and was not able to return to Munich until the third performance of the opera. 'Wagner was very glad to see me and thanked me personally for having come again, but I did not dare show him any compositions of mine even then.'

At a June choral competition in Linz his *Germanenzug* was first heard but he was upset at receiving only second prize. This was the occasion of his first meeting with the Viennese critic Eduard Hanslick, who at this time displayed nothing but friendliness, listening to Bruckner improvising at the organ, giving him advice, and presenting him with a signed photograph. Another meeting this year was with Liszt, in Pest, where he heard *St Elizabeth*. He subsequently met Berlioz in Vienna at a performance of *La Damnation de Faust*. How Bruckner fared in the company of these sophisticated arch-romantics is left to our imagination.

Work on the C minor Symphony continued into 1866, and his sister 'Nani' came to live with him in Linz, providing him with much needed company. He pursued two girls in the course of the year: Josephine Lang, who was seventeen and who rejected him because of the difference in their ages—which filled him with dismay—and Henriette Reiter, a 'lovely, dear girl' aged eighteen. With Henriette he inquired into all the details of her family position, social standing and financial status so as to approach marriage with her in the most business-like way, but the approach, as ever, was doomed to failure. He heard Beethoven's Ninth Symphony at this time and completed his own C minor Symphony (No. 1, 1866) and, in November, the second of his great Mass settings, in E minor, commissioned by Bishop Rudigier. A combination of overwork, fears for the future, anxieties about gaining recognition as an artist, and frustrated attempts at love led to severe depression and a total nervous collapse. He was admitted on 8 May 1867 to a sanatorium at Bad Kreuzen, and his letters from there show that this was a time of grave crisis. He spoke of impending madness, threatened suicide and regarded himself as utterly forsaken by the world. He also developed numeromania—an obsessive, neurotic condition which impelled him to count the leaves on trees, grains of sand, the stars, logs in a woodpile, and so on. His friend Frau Betty Mayfeld, who was staying at the sanatorium for a water-cure, could not wear one of her dresses as Bruckner started to count the pearls on it whenever he met her. Later in life these symptoms were to recur, and in his scores Bruckner meticulously numbered every bar and added up phrase-groups. Bishop Rudigier sent a priest to look after him. In a letter to Weinwurm of 19 June even the punctuation reveals his excitement and anxiety:

> Whatever you think or may have thought—or whatever you may have heard!—! It was not laziness!—It was much more than that!!!—!; it was a condition of utter degeneration and loneliness—total collapse of nerves and exhaustion!! I was in the most appalling state; you are the only person to hear of this—please keep quiet about it. In a little while I should have been a victim—lost. Doctor Fadinger of Linz told me that I could by now have been possessed by madness. God be thanked! He has saved me in time. . . . I am not permitted to play anything or study or work. Only think what a fate! What a wretched man I am! Herbeck sent me the score of my vocal Mass[4] and of the symphony[5] without writing a word. Are they as bad as that? Please find out. Write to me, dear friend!

On 8 August he left the sanatorium quite restored and relaxed. He applied for a lectureship in harmony and counterpoint at Vienna University, and again to the *Hofkapelle* for a position. In the latter application he made the extraordinary suggestion: 'Moreover I could be employed as a secretary and teacher in the principal schools, as I have served as a teacher for fourteen years.' Both applications were rejected, to Bruckner's great disappointment, but Johann Herbeck decided that he should be appointed professor of harmony and counterpoint at the Vienna Conservatory to succeed Simon Sechter, who had died on 10 September. Meanwhile, on 16 January 1868, Bruckner was reappointed conductor of the *Liedertafel 'Frohsinn'* and from September 1867 until September of the following year wrote his third great Mass, in F minor, which was the last work of his Linz period. A Phrygian 'Pange lingua' and an offertory, 'Inveni David,' also belong to 1868. Bruckner had requested a work from Wagner for the *Liedertafel* centenary concert on 4 April. Not having a suitable original work, Wagner wrote a friendly letter suggesting the last section of his newly completed *Die Meistersinger von Nürnberg*, and so Hans Sachs's famous solo at the end

---

[4] In E minor.   [5] In C minor, No. 1.

Fig. 2 Bruckner conducting: silhouette by Otto Böhler

of Act 3, and the final chorus, were first heard in Linz under the baton of Anton Bruckner along with his own *Vaterlandsliebe* (1866).

At Easter 1868 he was officially offered Sechter's old post as professor of organ-playing, counterpoint and 'General-bass' at the Vienna Conservatory. Just as when he moved from St Florian to Linz, he became anxious, indecisive, and afraid. He was dependent on his good salary at Linz and had been promised a pension for his old age. He wrote some pitiful letters including one to Herbeck in which he threatened to 'leave the world', and another to Bülow, requesting his help and that of Wagner to secure him a well-paid court or theatre post at Munich. He made a renewed attempt at obtaining the conductorship of the Salzburg *Dommusikverein* but was merely offered honorary membership.

On 9 May his Symphony in C minor (No. 1) was first performed at Linz under his own baton. Despite an inadequate performance and an inadequate audience (the bridge over the Danube had collapsed the previous day, distracting the populace) the occasion was a success. Mayfeld praised the work in the *Linzer Zietung* and Hanslick, so far loyal, wrote in the Vienna press: 'There are rumours that Bruckner is to join the staff of the Vienna Conservatory. If these should be correct, we may well congratulate the institution.' But Bruckner was still disturbed about the idea. Only when Herbeck had succeeded in raising his salary from 600 to 800 florins, when he was also appointed *Expektant* organist at the *Hofkapelle,* and when the authorities at Linz promised to keep his job open as a line of retreat did he move, with his sister 'Nani', in the summer of 1868, to Höhne-Haus, Währingerstrasse 41, Vienna.

4

Vienna

When Bruckner arrived in Vienna, it was the heyday of Johann Strauss the younger, and the city was a backcloth of elegant boulevards for a sparkling society and for frivolous gaiety, waltzes, and operettas. It was also the home of Brahms, whom most of the musical circles in the city, including the mightiest of the critics, Hanslick, regarded as the heir of Beethoven. The antipode of Brahms was Wagner, and after him Liszt. The two hostile camps were quite irreconcilable. But during his first winter in Vienna, Bruckner attended Hanslick's lectures at Vienna University on the history of music.

Duties at the *Konservatorium der Gesellschaft der Musikfreunde* began on 1 October 1868. Bruckner had an easy, lively method of teaching, with the gift of presenting an academic point in an enjoyable, even amusing way.[1] But he was as strict and severe as Sechter when it came to the standards he expected of his students, and he allowed no free composition during the course. He was certainly one of the greatest composers of the century to apply himself to the teaching of harmony and counterpoint, and no one could have been better equipped for the task. His first pupils included the young virtuoso pianist Vladimir de Pachmann, the future Bruckner interpreter Felix Mottl, and, shortly after, Guido Adler. Other pupils of the Vienna years who attained distinction included his future editors Franz Schalk and Ferdinand Löwe, his future biographer August Göllerich, and the writers Ernst Decsey and Friedrich Eckstein who were to leave memorable accounts of this unforgettable teacher, the violinist Fritz Kreisler, the pianist August Stradal, the conductors Rudolf Krzyzanowski, Emil Paur, and Arthur Nikisch, the composers Friedrich Klose, Cyrill Hynais, František Marschner, Ernest Schelling, Franz Schmidt, and Emile Jacques-Dalcroze, and the organist Hans Rott. Rott was a declared favourite of Bruckner's, a very fine organist, composer, and friend of Mahler. (Tragically, he died insane in 1884.) Bruckner soon had another rise in salary, and in December 1868 the Ministry of Education awarded him 500 florins for 'the composition of major symphonic works'.

[1] He called the diminished seventh chord the 'musical Orient Express' because it can take one so quickly to faraway places.

His post at the *Hofkapelle* was an honorary one, and in addition to duties as organist he became vice-librarian and second singing-teacher to the choristers. He was not an outstanding success at the *Hofkapelle*, was rarely asked to play on great occasions and found little opportunity to show his skills as an improviser there. It was only in later years that the emperor and his family expressly requested him to play at important private celebrations. In fact Bruckner never excelled as an accompanist of choirs. Liszt complained of his dragging accompaniment at a performance of one of his oratorios. There were some unfavourable criticisms of his organ-playing, although these were more than likely due to musical politics. He was but an average pianist and violinist, he had gained a good deal of experience as a choral singer, he was a competent conductor of choirs, but largely unsuccessful as an orchestral conductor and his performances of his own symphonies suffered because of this.

The close of 1868 saw some rehearsals, under Herbeck, of the F minor Mass, but these were poorly attended, and the first performance of the work did not materialize for three years. From January of the next year Bruckner worked on the D minor symphony, No. 0 ('die Nullte'), and continued this task until September. Like the early 'study symphony' in F minor, it was excluded from his official canon of symphonies, but a year before his death he bequeathed the work to a museum in Linz. The first movement is the boldest and the finest and surely must have been composed after the First Symphony in C minor. Indeed Bruckner's autograph calls the work Symphony 'No. 2'. Some scholars, adhering to the belief that this 1869 work was a revision of one from 1863–4, explain this by regarding the F minor 'study symphony' as 'No. 1'. Clearly there is much confusion here, which is unlikely to be resolved unless autograph material of an earlier version of 'No. 0' or documents relating to it turn up. As the first of his C minor symphonies is referred to in one letter[2] as 'No. 2', and as the second was originally marked 'No. 3', the situation may well bewilder the newcomer to Bruckner. Put most simply (and rejecting an earlier version of 'No. 0') one can tabulate his first five symphonies with their original and final numberings thus:

Date	Symphony	Projected No.	Final No.
1863	F minor	No. 1(?)	—
1866	C minor	No. 2	No. 1
1869	D minor	No. 2	No. 0
1872	C minor	No. 3	No. 2
1872–3	D minor	No. 3	No. 3

[2] To R. Weinwurm, 29 January 1865.

I find it difficult to accept that much of No. 0 was written before No. 1. From the above table some approximate idea can be deduced as to when Bruckner determined upon his final numberings and when he decided not to include the 1869 work in his numbered canon (i.e. by the time he began work on the Third Symphony in D minor in 1872, as its numbering was never in question). About this time, Dessoff, the conductor of the Vienna Philharmonic Orchestra, rejected the First Symphony on account of its wildness and daring, and he thought little more of 'die Nullte', work on which was interrupted by an invitation to visit France in April 1869.

Hanslick must take the credit for the choice of Bruckner to take part in a series of recitals on a new organ in the Church of St Epvre, Nancy. At Nancy his playing of Bach and his improvisation made such an impression that he was asked to go on to Paris, where he played on the organ of Notre Dame before a distinguished audience which included Saint-Saëns, Franck, Auber, Gounod, and Ambroise Thomas. His Paris improvisations were remembered with admiration in later years. On his way home he stayed in Wels and here another young lady, Karoline Rabl, caught his eye and awoke his longing for marriage.

The triumphs in France were followed on 29 September by a moving première of the Mass in E minor outside Linz Cathedral, and one of his most beautiful motets of this year, 'Locus iste', was first heard in Linz in October. He was made an honorary citizen of Ansfelden and an honorary member of the Linz *Liedertafel*. His next symphonic essay consisted of sketches for a Symphony in B flat major—the only example of his use of a major key for a symphonic work at this time. But the plan was to give way to work on Symphony No. 2, although the sketches provided material for both this and the Fourth Symphony.

In 1870 Bruckner's sister 'Nani' died, after looking after him for four years. Soon he took a housekeeper, Katharina Kachelmayr ('Frau Kathi'), who stayed with him until his death. She cared for him in a motherly fashion, and although they often squabbled, her services were invaluable to him. He was awarded a further grant of 400 florins from the Ministry of Education, and towards the end of the year was appointed teacher of piano, organ, and theory at the teacher-training college of St Anna, which raised his salary by 540 florins but gave him less time for creative work. He also took private pupils.

He was selected to represent Austria in a series of six recitals on the new Henry Willis organ at the Royal Albert Hall, London, in August 1871. The English press was more reserved in its enthusiasm than the French, but the result of the Albert Hall appearances was a further five recitals at the Crystal Palace. The *Morning Advertiser* of 1 September spoke of his playing of Bach and Mendelssohn as 'truly excellent . . . leaving nothing to be desired', and went on:

Herr Bruckner excels in his improvisation. You will find great easiness and abundance of ideas, and the ingenious method by which such an idea is carried out is very remarkable. The London public has fully acknowledged Herr Bruckner's perfect execution and may have expressed a hope that this first visit may not be the last. We join in. Bruckner may publish some of his most successful compositions for the benefit and enjoyment of the musical public, who, we are sure, would be very pleased to become better acquainted with the works of this thorough artist.

The highlight of at least one recital was an improvisation 'on English melodies' including *God Save the Queen*. He told Mayfeld in a letter from his hotel in Finsbury Square that he had played at one concert before an audience of 70,000 and had to give encores, and that the conductor, August Manns, had asked him to come again to London and introduce himself as a composer. This came to nothing, and a planned series of recitals in the major towns of England for the following year never materialized. Yet Bruckner frequently longed to return to England, and in moments of trial in Vienna seriously thought of doing so.

A silly scandal awaited him on returning to Vienna. In his rough, straightforward Upper Austrian dialect he had innocently addressed a girl in the college of St Anna in a familiar way ('lieber Schatz') and a great fuss had been made. Bruckner was upset and asked to be relieved of his duties in the female section of the college, which meant losing some of his salary. Characteristically he was not calmed until Hellmesberger, the director of the Conservatory, supplied him with a testimonial confirming perfect discipline in his classes there. He began his Symphony No. 2 (like the First, in C minor) in October 1871 and revised the F minor Mass for its first performance at the *Augustiner-kirche* on 16 June 1872. He conducted himself, and the work was enthusiastically received. Herbeck commented: 'I know only two Masses—this one and Beethoven's Missa Solemnis.' Brahms was present and was deeply moved, Hanslick gave it some praise in the *Neue Freie Presse*, and Liszt thought very highly of it.

Work progressed on the Second Symphony, especially when Bruckner found time to make one of his regular visits to a retreat in Upper Austria. He completed it on 11 September 1872 and immediately sent it to Dessoff, who rehearsed it with the Vienna Philharmonic and sent it back with the verdict, 'unplayable'. Despite this, Bruckner pressed on with another symphony, No. 3 in D minor, which occupied him from the autumn of 1872 until 31 December 1873. Armed with this manuscript and other scores, he set off in the summer for Marienbad and Karlsbad, finally reaching Bayreuth in September 1873, where he determined to meet Wagner again. Wagner was busy working on the *Ring* and at first tried to get rid of the persistent intruder. The famous meeting is best described in Bruckner's own words:[3]

[3] Letter to Hans von Wolzogen, September 1884.

I said: 'Master, I have no right to rob you of even five minutes, but I am convinced that the highly acute glance of the Master would only have to see the themes, and the Master would know what to think of it all.' Then the Master said to me, 'Very well then, come along!' And he took me into the drawing room and looked at the Second Symphony. 'Very nice', he said, but none the less it did not seem bold enough for him (at that time the Viennese had made me very timid), and he took the Third (D minor) and with the words, 'Look! Look! I say! I say!' he went through the entire first part (commenting particularly on the trumpet[4]) and then he said: 'Leave this work here; after lunch [it was then twelve o'clock] I will have another look at it.' I thought, dare I ask him before he says I may? Very shyly and with a pounding heart I then said to the Master: 'Master! there is something in my heart that I lack courage to speak of.' The Master said: 'Out with it! You know how I like you!' Then I presented my petition (that is the intention of dedicating the work to him), but only if the Master was more or less satisfied, as I did not wish to do sacrilege to his most celebrated name. The Master said: 'This evening at five o'clock you are invited to Wahnfried[5]; you will see me then; after I have had a good look at the D minor Symphony we can discuss the matter.'

Afterwards Wagner told him that he accepted the dedication with 'immense pleasure' and they drank beer together and Wagner showed him his grave, whereupon Bruckner knelt and prayed. Overwhelmed with the result of the meeting and feeling the effects of too much beer, Bruckner could not remember on the following day which of the two works Wagner had accepted, so he sent a note to him:

Symphony in D minor where the trumpet begins the theme?
Anton Bruckner.

Wagner wrote hastily underneath this:
Yes! Yes! Best wishes!
Richard Wagner.

After his Bayreuth visit Bruckner joined the *Akademischer Richard Wagner-Verein* and this, together with his pride at the composer's recognition of him, led to his growing reputation in Vienna as a Wagnerian.

On 26 October he conducted the Vienna Philharmonic in the first performance of Symphony No. 2—a concert arranged by Herbeck who had at length found a willing patron in the person of Prince Johann Liechtenstein. The evening included a much-praised organ improvisation by the composer. Ludwig Speidel wrote most favourably about the work and so on the whole did Hanslick, who took the opportunity, however,

---

[4] Thus Wagner's nickname for Bruckner—the Trumpet.
[5] Wagner's villa was almost complete though not yet occupied by the family. On the afternoon of this visit his wife Cosima was sitting to the sculptor Kietz who had set up studio in the house and who in his memoirs wrote amusingly of Bruckner's excitement and subsequent befuddlement (Gustav Adolph Kietz, *Richard Wagner in den Jahren 1842–49 und 1873–75* (Dresden, 1905). English trans. by Stewart Spencer in *Wagner*, 16/3, London, Sept. 1995.)

Fig. 3 Bruckner's note to Wagner and 'the Master's' reply

to point out its 'Wagnerian' derivation. Afterwards Bruckner wrote to the orchestra offering the dedication of the work. They never replied. The Third Symphony was completed in its first form and contained a number of quotations from Wagner's works (namely the *Ring* and *Tristan* in the first two movements). Its writing had given Bruckner much joy. It was also to bring him more pain than any other work and he began making 'extensive improvements' to it as early as 1874. Two days elapsed between the completion of the Third Symphony and the first sketches for a Fourth, in E flat major, on 2 January 1874, and this work was in turn complete by 22 November.

It was a year of unsuccessful attempts at improving his fortunes. When his post at the college of St Anna was terminated for economic reasons, he applied for a government grant, renewed his 1867 application for a lectureship in the university, and tried to find backing for a move to England. All these attempts failed, but the university application has some interest as applications for a music lectureship went to the Dean of the Music Faculty—Eduard Hanslick. Hanslick felt that there was no need for such a post as his own lectures covered the fields of harmony and counterpoint adequately, and he made this clear in his reports to the State authorities. He also made some barbed attacks on Bruckner, who persisted and wrote no fewer than three further applications, each followed by a clear 'No' from Hanslick, who wrote:

In order to be spared the necessity of enlarging on this point I permit myself the request that the honourable committee of professors should give attention to the remarkable style of Bruckner's application.

I find in this application no facts that call for a revision of my previous views respecting this matter. There is, furthermore, no evidence present to show that Herr Bruckner has ever produced striking results as a teacher of composition.

Bruckner was encouraged in these applications by Karl Edler von Stremayr, Minister of Education, and a professor, August Göllerich (father of Bruckner's biographer-to-be), and in December there was even a mention of the affair in a newspaper.

But poor Bruckner was a 'Wagnerian'. Wagner, on a visit to Vienna, ignored a committee of welcome at the station and went up to Bruckner saying: 'When will the symphony be performed?', and then turning to the others: 'Bruckner! He is my man!' Since Bruckner's real interest in the dramatic content of Wagner's music dramas appears to have been slight and Wagner's real interest in Bruckner's symphonies was nil, this is a state of affairs sad to contemplate. That Wagner never helped Bruckner personally is explicable, surely forgivable, given his multitude of cares over Bayreuth. He could, however, have encouraged other conductors in his circle to take up Bruckner's works (most of them did later); or he could have used his influence with publishers to have Bruckner's scores printed; and he could have included some reference to Bruckner in his writings. He did none of these and thus appears to have been merely condescending to Bruckner (perhaps for diplomatic reasons) and like Liszt may have found his extreme adoration and obsequiousness somewhat fulsome. But a word of praise from Wagner could put right any venom of Hanslick's, and so Bruckner continued to strive to establish his place in Vienna, where all the signs indicated he was swimming against a powerful tide.

5

Awakened mastery

The story of Bruckner's life now becomes the story of symphonies—a story highlighted by achievements, triumphs, and honours, and yet darkened by the disappointments and problems that these massive works brought in their wake. Dessoff promised in October 1874 to perform the Third Symphony and shortly after went back on his word with the excuse that the programme was full. In the following year he rehearsed the newly completed Fourth Symphony and returned it with the opinion that only the first movement might merit a performance. And yet Bruckner had no hesitation about embarking on a new symphony, No. 5 in B flat major. In this he was finally to master the new and vast concept of symphonic structure that he had been forging in the Third and Fourth Symphonies. Ironically it was the only one of his eight completed mature symphonies of which he was never to hear a note played.

On 12 January 1875 he wrote to Mayfeld complaining of his difficulties in arranging a performance of the Third Symphony, of his poor financial state, and of the dearth of pupils:

> You will now realize how serious my situation has become. I would happily settle abroad if only I were assured an existence. Where shall I turn? Nothing could have persuaded me to come to Vienna if I had only had a hint of what was ahead. It would be simple for my enemies to force me out of the Conservatory. I am really surprised that they have not already done so. . . . My life has been robbed of every joy—through pure malice. How gladly I would return to my old post at Linz! If only I had gone to England then!

He strove once more in August to persuade the Philharmonic to play the Third Symphony but was refused.

Meanwhile he had applied yet again for a university lectureship, and this time, despite Hanslick's opposition, was appointed in an honorary capacity and gave his inaugural lecture on 25 November 1875, while still at work on the Symphony No. 5. Bruckner enjoyed his work at the university with his 'gaudeamuses', as he called his students. His teaching methods have been preserved in books by his pupils, Klose, Eckstein, and Schwanzara. His clear, systematic method was to some extent influ-

Fig. 4 Bruckner teaching: caricature by Grandi

enced by Sechter's teaching[1] and he never taught 'real' composition or introduced the new, creative thoughts of Liszt or Wagner into his classes. He was an admirable teacher of the fundamental elements of musical construction and he was liked for his individuality and warm personality. Many of his pupils at this time became his future champions and he delighted to spend evenings with groups of them over beer and supper at an inn or restaurant, when the conversation no doubt ranged over new and progressive ideas in music. His young adherents at this time included a teenage boy, Gustav Mahler, who became a friend and later interpreter, although he never studied with him. Arnold Schoenberg is known to have attended some of Bruckner's lectures. Thus the author of the *Harmonielehre* might almost be viewed as a 'grand-pupil' of Sechter's. In turn, Alban Berg knew his Bruckner well and

[1] for example the 'interdominant' or 'interpolated root' theory. In progressions of triads with no common note, an imaginary, intermediate root harmony is postulated, so D–E is D–B–E. Schoenberg stressed this idea in his teaching of step-wise progressions.

31

quotes from the Mass in D minor in Act 3 of *Wozzeck*. Schoenberg also made a chamber version of the Symphony No. 7.

In 1876 the three great Masses were all slightly revised and the Fifth Symphony was completed in May. The Second Symphony had received another performance in February with Bruckner conducting. This concert had also been arranged by Herbeck but he pressed Bruckner into making a number of drastic cuts, and this set an unfortunate precedent for the revisions of later years. The work had a mixed reception and while the audience applauded vigorously, one critic called Bruckner 'a fool and a half', and Hanslick wrote a hostile review criticizing the 'lack of form'. This may be the reason for further revisions of the Second Symphony in 1877. During these years he regularly visited Upper Austria in the summer, often staying at St Florian, and in August 1876 he attended the first performance of the *Ring* at Bayreuth and renewed his friendship with Wagner.

In January 1877 he applied unsuccessfully for the post of conductor at the church *am Hof*. He moved during the year to a rent-free fourth-floor flat at Hessgasse 7, on the corner of the Schottenring, in the house of an admirer, Dr Anton Ölzelt-Newin, whom he had met on a visit to Klosterneuburg, and he stayed this prestigious address until 1895. In this spacious apartment, which had a fine view of the city, he lived in simplicity. His bedroom contained only an English brass bed, presented by his pupils ('my luxury'), some portraits and a bust of himself. The other, blue-walled, room contained his piano, harmonium, armchair, worktable, and chest of drawers. In the hall he made a collection of laurel wreaths awarded to him, and stacks of music and manuscript paper lay all around.

The sorry history of the Third Symphony continued. During 1876–7 it was again revised and the Wagner quotations (from *Tristan* and *Die Walküre*) were removed. He completed the revision on 28 April 1877. Herbeck planned to conduct a performance of it, but died suddenly on 28 October. The death of this ardent enthusiast was a grievous blow to Bruckner. However, August Göllerich and his son (Bruckner's pupil) arranged for the performance to take place on 16 December, but Bruckner had to conduct. Before the concert he wrote to a sympathetic critic in Berlin, Wilhelm Tappert:

> Our Philharmonic is absolutely antagonistic to the 'New Order' in music. I shall never submit any of my works to them again, for they have rejected my offerings repeatedly. How Richter can remain on the best terms with Wagner's bitterest opponents is truly amazing to me. Alas, I too have come to know him as the arch-liar he is. Only recently have many of Wagner's statements become clear to me. I implore you not to be turned against me by the malicious statements that are made about me.

The première of Symphony No. 3 came at the end of a long programme and was an almost unmitigated disaster, partly because its scale was beyond Bruckner's conducting ability. The audience left the hall in growing numbers and when the last note sounded, and the orchestra had fled the platform, 'that fraction of the public which had remained to the end consoled him for the flight of the rest', to put it in Hanslick's words. Hanslick imagined the work as 'a vision of Beethoven's Ninth becoming friendly with Wagner's Valkyries and finishing up trampled under their hooves'. Bruckner was in a state of shattered emotion and refused to listen to the consolations of his faithful students. Then, amazingly, Theodor Rättig, a publisher, who had been to rehearsals of the work and had witnessed the *débâcle*, went to him and offered to publish the symphony. So, in 1878, a symphony of his was published with parts, and in a piano-duet reduction prepared by Mahler and Krzyzanowsky. But the dark day of 16 December affected Bruckner to the extent that almost no composition followed for a year; he further revised the Third Symphony, thoroughly revised the Fourth, touched up the Fifth, and allowed the Third to be published in a cut form. The only work of 1878 of lasting merit was a motet, 'Tota pulchra es Maria', one of his best small liturgical works, dedicated to Bishop Rudigier on his silver jubilee.

Bruckner was now appointed a full member of the *Hofkapelle* with an annual salary of 800 florins. Also in 1878 a fine organ was built by Mauracher at the Benedictine monastery of Kremsmünster. Bruckner was no stranger there, but this instrument and the devoted friendship of his pupil Father Rafael (Oddo) Loidal (dedicatee of the setting of 'Christus factus est' WAB 11), drew him to Kremsmünster more and more in the later years. The monastery had had associations with Haydn, Mozart, and Schubert, and its distinguished library was particularly noted for motets of the early seventeenth century. In December Bruckner began his only mature work of chamber music, a String Quintet in F major. Joseph Hellmesberger had asked him for a quartet, but Bruckner preferred the richer possibilities of quintet writing. The work was finished on 12 July 1879, shortly after the revision of the Fourth Symphony was complete; and in the same year appeared two motets, the eight-part 'Christus factus est' (WAB 10) and 'Os justi', the latter set in the Lydian mode. Hellmesberger found the Scherzo of the Quintet 'too difficult' and this movement was replaced by an Intermezzo (completed in December), although in the end the Scherzo was retained.

The lessons in string-writing gained in the Quintet benefited the Symphony No. 6 in A major, begun on 24 September. But work on this was interrupted in 1880 by a further revision of the Fourth Symphony, including the writing of a new and dramatic finale. Bruckner applied for the conductorship of the *Wiener Männergesangverein*, but his standing in Vienna was not yet impressive enough for him to be considered even for this. On 6 June Hellmesberger (who so far had not dared perform the Quintet) mounted a performance of the D minor Mass, which he considered a true masterpiece, in Vienna. Then Bruckner took a holiday, visiting St Florian, Oberammergau for the Passion Play, Munich, and, finally, Switzerland, where he played organs in Geneva, Freiburg, Berne, Zurich, and Lucerne. Several pretty girls excited his attentions on this trip. At Oberammergau he was attracted to one of the 'daughters of Jerusalem', the seventeen-year-old Marie Bartl. He met her at the stage door, was introduced to her family and corresponded with her for about a year. Then she stopped writing.

On returning to Vienna via St Florian, Bruckner suffered from an ailment in the feet and legs which troubled him considerably in after years. He settled down to serious work on the Sixth Symphony, and received, after many applications, the consent of the university for a payment of 800 florins for his academic work. In February 1881 Symphony No. 4 was first performed, under Richter. At a rehearsal for this concert occurred the famous and rather touching incident when the overjoyed Bruckner came up to Richter, pressed a small tip into his hand and said: 'Take this and drink my health with a glass of beer.' Richter wore the

Fig. 5 Bruckner and Richter: silhouettes by Otto Böhler

coin on his watch chain ever after. At the concert itself (on 20 February) Hans von Bülow participated, conducting his symphonic poem *Des Sängers Fluch* and playing Beethoven's Fourth Piano Concerto. But Bruckner's Fourth outshone even Bülow (possibly influencing the latter's marked lack of future interest in Bruckner). The performance under Richter was a great victory for Bruckner and even the most unfriendly sections of the press gave him credit. The *Neue Freie Presse* spoke of 'an unusual success'. In May he began the first draft of a Te Deum, on 3 September the Sixth Symphony was completed, and in less than three weeks the Seventh Symphony in E major was under way. Bruckner related that the first subject was given to him in dream by Ignaz Dorn (who had died in May 1872).

Still Hellmesberger was too nervous to perform the Quintet, to Bruckner's disappointment. But Franz Schalk joined with the Winkler Quartet as second viola and gave a performance of it (without the finale) at a private concert of the *Akademischer Richard Wagner-Verein* in December 1881. Ludwig Speidel, who attended rehearsals, enthused about the remarkable freedom and ease with which Bruckner utilized the whole tonal spectrum and praised especially the polyphonic warmth of the Adagio. The Masses in D minor and E minor were now revised for the last time, the F minor Mass was heard at the *Hofkapelle*, and an infatuation with a young girl with a fine contralto voice brought forth a setting of the 'Ave Maria'.

In July he visited Bayreuth for the first performance of *Parsifal*. It was his last meeting with his beloved master, and he described it later to Hans von Wolzogen of Bayreuth:

> In 1882, when he was already suffering from severe illness, he once took my hand, saying: 'Don't worry. I myself will perform the symphony and all of your works.' Moved, I could only exclaim: 'Oh, Master!' Then he asked: 'Have you heard *Parsifal*? How do you like it?' And then while he still held my hand, I knelt before him and pressing it to my lips, said: 'Oh Master, I worship you!' Then he said: 'Be calm—Bruckner. Goodnight!!!' These were the Master's last words to me. On the following day he sat behind me at the *Parsifal* performance and I was scolded for applauding too loudly. Herr Baron, please take great care of all this! My most cherished testament!!!—Until yonder, above!!![2]

Returning through his familiar Upper Austria, he worked earnestly at Symphony No. 7. A mysterious 'Englishman' appeared in this year and extorted a sum of money from him, having raised his hopes for a Cambridge doctorate. Bruckner heard the Sixth Symphony under Jahn in rehearsal, but only the middle two movements reached the public ear on 11 February 1883. A pupil of Bruckner's, Emil Lamberg, reported that while Brahms joined in the colossal ovation, 'Hanslick sat there, frigid and immobile, like a sphinx'. The Quintet had two performances

---

[2] The collected edition of Bruckner's *Briefe* gives 1884 as the date of this letter.

that year. On 13 February, as Bruckner was completing the Adagio of his Seventh Symphony, Wagner died in Venice. The closing pages of the movement are Bruckner's tribute to his memory. In August he journeyed to Bayreuth to visit Wagner's grave and at St Florian, on 5 September, he completed the symphony which was soon to alter his fame and fortunes.

6

Growing fame, illness, and death

The major choral work of Bruckner's Vienna period, his Te Deum, was written in its final form between 28 September 1883 and 7 March 1884. It is in many ways a summation of the man: his mastery of choral writing, his individuality in symphonic integration, and above all the intensity of his religious fervour.

The Quintet had several performances and was also published during 1884. On the whole it drew praise from the critics, including the Brahmans, but one critic, while praising the Quintet itself, saw fit to call Bruckner

> the greatest living musical peril, a sort of tonal anti-Christ. The violent nature of the man is not written in his face, for his expression indicates at most the small soul of an every-day Kapellmeister. Yet he composes nothing but high treason, revolution and murder. His work is absolutely devoid of art or reason. . . . His music has the fragrance of heavenly roses, but it is poisonous with the sulphurs of hell.[1]

As well as completing two motets in this year, the 'greatest living musical peril' began his greatest symphony, No. 8 in C minor. He paid a visit to Prague, and on his return met Liszt, to whom he offered the dedication of the Second Symphony. Liszt formally accepted, but left his hotel in a hurry, forgetting to take the score with him. When Bruckner learned this he was hurt and withdrew the dedication. During the year he met Hugo Wolf, at that time critic of the *Wiener Salonblatt*, who immediately became an ardent, indeed vehement protagonist for him. After a summer visiting Bayreuth, Munich, Kremsmünster, and his beloved St Florian (which he habitually visited several times a year), he celebrated his sixtieth birthday in Vöcklabruck with his only surviving sister, Rosalia, and the town band honoured the occasion publicly. While there he worked on the Eighth Symphony and took a fancy to a young village girl to whom he brought some flowers each day. She was replaced in his heart, however, in the following spring by another teenager, Marie Denmar.

[1] Max Kalbeck in the *Neue Freie Presse*; quoted in Göllerich–Auer IV/2, pp. 249 ff.

The première of the Seventh Symphony unlocked a new door in Bruckner's path, and he strode on accompanied by a growing momentum of public acclaim. The performance on 30 December was given in Leipzig by the Gewandhaus Orchestra under Nikisch, and it established his reputation not only in Germany but also internationally. A Leipzig critic wrote:

> One could see from the trembling of his lips and the sparkling moisture in his eyes how difficult it was for the old gentleman to suppress the deep emotion that he felt. His homely, honest countenance beamed with a warm inner happiness such as can appear only on the face of one who is too good-hearted to give way to bitterness even under the weight of most crushing circumstances. Having heard his music, and now seeing him in person, we asked ourselves in amazement, 'How is it possible that he could remain so long unknown to us?'

Herman Levi performed the work in March 1885, again with marked success, and it was also heard during that year in Dresden, Frankfurt, Utrecht, New York, and twice in The Hague. Liszt helped to organize and also attended a performance of its Adagio in Karlsruhe and was thereafter to work tirelessly to further Bruckner's name. Not long before his death Liszt was personally responsible for arranging a concert including the Quintet and the first and third movements of the Fourth Symphony in Sondershausen—a typically noble gesture from an artist whose own works were rarely heard and subject to marked animosity. The Vienna Philharmonic considered a performance of the Seventh Symphony, but Bruckner begged them not to proceed for fear that Hanslick and the Vienna press might destroy the advantage he had gained abroad. But Gutmann published the work for a fee of 1,000 florins, and King Ludwig II of Bavaria honoured Bruckner by accepting the dedication.

During 1885 he laboured at the Eighth Symphony, wrote two exquisite motets 'Ecce sacerdos' and 'Virga Jesse floruit', and conducted a première of the Te Deum in Vienna with two pianos substituted for orchestra. Two notable organ improvisations were also given. On 28 August, the feast of St Augustine, patron saint of St Florian, Bruckner gave a mighty rendering of themes from *Götterdämmerung* and from his sketched Eighth Symphony in the *Stiftkirche*; and on the feast of St Leopold, patron saint of Austria, gave a rousing improvisation on the *Kaiserlied* at Klosterneuburg. The emperor was present on the second of these occasions: as he entered to the sound of the organ he was reported to have stood still for a moment, then looked upwards and murmured, 'Ah, Bruckner!'. The same year saw, at last, a performance by Hellmesberger of the Quintet in Vienna, including the original Scherzo; and one of the E minor Mass in Linz. But persistent ailments began to trouble Bruckner, and a form of dropsy set in. These symptoms hampered his busy life, but they did not become acute until his last few years.

Though he applied unsuccessfully for a doctorate to the Universities of Philadelphia and Cincinnati, honours did come. He was decorated by the emperor with the Order of Franz-Josef in July 1886, received by him personally, and given a grant of 300 florins from the Imperial purse. He sat for portraits, and Fritz von Uhde honoured him in a way that moved him deeply, by using him as a model for one of the disciples in his painting of the 'Last Supper'. Performances occurred in growing numbers, Symphony No. 3 at Linz and The Hague, No. 4 at Sondershausen, and No. 7 at Graz, Hamburg, Cologne, Amsterdam, New York, Boston, and Chicago (in 1886); and in the next year No. 7 was heard in Berlin, Cologne, Budapest, twice in Dresden, and twice in London. The Te Deum performance was another victory (Vienna, 10 January 1886) and even Hanslick made some concessions.

However, the Vienna première of the Seventh Symphony was to justify Bruckner's nervousness about the critical reaction. While the performance under Richter (in March 1886) filled the audience with enthusiasm and secured a great ovation for the composer, Hanslick called the work 'unnatural, bombastic, sickly and decadent'. Brahms's official biographer, Kalbeck, said: 'It comes from the Nibelungen and goes to the devil', and Hanslick's polemical mouthpiece, Gustav Dömpke, declared that 'Bruckner composes like a drunkard'.

Bruckner visited Prague to play on a new organ, and journeyed with Levi, Mottl, Stradal, and Göllerich to Bayreuth in August. Liszt had just died, and Cosima Wagner invited him to take part in her father's funeral. He marked the occasion with a towering improvisation at the organ on themes from *Parsifal*.

Work on the Eighth Symphony continued until 1887, a year that also saw the publication of the Te Deum (financed by his pupil Friedrich Eckstein); a number of his smaller sacred works also appearing in print in these years. On 4 September he wrote to Hermann Levi: 'Hallelujah! At long last the Eighth is finished and my artistic father must be the first to know about it. . . . May it find grace!' Levi was a staunch champion of Bruckner, but he could not follow or comprehend this, the longest and most solemn of Bruckner's symphonic canvases. Not wishing to hurt Bruckner directly, he sent news of his failure to appreciate the work via Joseph Schalk. The viciousness of Hanslick's attacks, the fiasco of the première of the Third Symphony and the nervous collapse of his Linz years were nothing in comparison to the effect this information had on Bruckner. It marked the greatest setback of his creative career. He was in despair, many of his symptoms of neurosis reappeared, and he thought of suicide. The practical result of the rejection was the beginning of his most intensive and largely disastrous period of revisions, and the result of this in turn was that he never completed another symphony. Robert Simpson has pointed out[2] that but for these years of altering and

[2] See *The Essence of Bruckner*, pp. 64, 212, and 230.

rewriting, he would probably have finished his Ninth Symphony (sketches for which date from the month of Levi's rejection) and might have begun a Tenth.

The revision of the Eighth Symphony began in October 1887 and was not complete until 10 March 1890. Bruckner's life was still full of teaching duties and he allowed himself to be aided in his task of revision by his pupils.[3] His own creative judgement was thus influenced by the opinions of these well-meaning friends, and countless alterations and small details that would never have survived his critical eye under ordinary conditions found their way into the pages of these revisions. This is particularly true in the case of the first published versions of his symphonies, all of which are to a greater or lesser extent spurious. A completely new version of the Third Symphony was worked out during the revision of the Eighth. Some years earlier Bruckner had been persuaded to revise and shorten the Third Symphony and had in fact begun this task, asking the publisher to re-engrave fifty-two pages of the score. Mahler then persuaded him that the revision was superfluous and the plates were scrapped, but now the revising mania could not be checked. Two days after the Eighth was completed a new version of the First Symphony was begun and was in turn completed in April 1891. The F minor Mass was revised from 1890 to 1893.

In 1889 the Fourth Symphony was published as a result of an appeal for finances by Levi,[4] and in the next year the revised Third Symphony appeared in print, with expenses defrayed by the emperor. Also in 1889 the first payment of an annual grant from a group of Austrian industrialists was made to Bruckner and he was created an honorary member of the *Richard Wagner-Verein*. In the autumn a meeting with Brahms was arranged by friends of the two composers in order to bring the two men closer together. This aim was never realized, but although the meeting at a Viennese restaurant, the 'Roten Igel', started coldly and formally, the ice was broken when they discovered that they shared an enthusiasm for traditional Austrian dishes. They spent a convivial evening over smoked ham and dumplings but never entered into any debate about music. Although Bruckner had written in February 1885 complaining of Brahms's 'almost insulting behaviour' towards him, it seems that Brahms, who was a master of impoliteness when he chose to be rude, always greeted Bruckner with respect and civility. He never indulged in the public displays of vitriol that Hanslick regarded as his pious duty. In private, Brahms called Bruckner's symphonies 'symphonic boaconstrictors' and 'a swindle that will be forgotten in a few years'. Bruckner in turn said he preferred a Johann Strauss waltz to a Brahms symphony. Strauss returned the compliment, incidentally, and sent a telegram to

[3] For details see Chapter 9.
[4] Bruckner wrote to the publisher Gutmann requesting that not a note of the parts be altered. His request was ignored.

Bruckner after the first performance of the Seventh Symphony: 'I am deeply moved. It was one of the strongest impressions in my life.'

In the spring of 1890 Bruckner suffered from chronic catarrh of the larynx and his nervous condition further deteriorated. In the autumn he was excused from his duties as organ professor at the Conservatory and in December wrote the only work of the entire 1887–91 revision period, a small male-voice chorus, *Träumen und Wachen*. On 21 December the new version of the Third Symphony was heard in Vienna under Richter and received a great ovation.

The year 1891 (the year of Bruckner's retirement from the Conservatory) saw several triumphs. An ovation almost unprecedented in Berlin musical annals greeted him at a performance of the Te Deum, conducted by Siegfried Ochs, in May. While there he met a hotel chambermaid, Ida Buhz, who actually offered to marry him. Meetings with her family (both then and in 1894) ensued, but in 1895 he turned down the idea of a betrothal when it became clear that she would not change her Lutheran faith to become a Catholic. He visited Bayreuth in August for the first *Festspielhaus* performance of *Tannhäuser*, and at the Mozart festival at Salzburg offered to marry the young Minna Reischl, but her parents opposed the match, although a lively correspondence continued until his death. On 30 October the Upper Austrian Diet voted him an honorary stipend of 400 florins, and on 7 November he received the honour that meant most of all to him—an honorary Ph.D. of the University of Vienna, the first time the award had been made to a musician. Bruckner was so moved at the ceremony that he was unable to reply coherently, ending his confused speech: 'I cannot find words to thank you as I wish, but if there was an organ here I could tell you.' At a gala reception for 3,000 people a month later, in his honour, Dr Adolf Exner spoke the words: 'I, Rector Magnificus of the University of Vienna, bow humbly before the former assistant teacher of Windhaag.'

On 13 December 1891 the première of the Symphony No. 1 in its new version took place under Richter, and in the following year Psalm 150, in the exultant vein of the Te Deum, was written and performed, as were a secular piece, *Das deutsche Lied*, and the last of his motets, 'Vexilla regis'. Bruckner's last visit to Bayreuth was in August 1892, when he prayed daily at Wagner's grave. In the confusion of his arrival, he lost his sketches for the Ninth Symphony, but after some anxious hours they were found at the police station and work continued. On 18 December the Eighth Symphony, dedicated to the emperor, was heard in Vienna under Richter, and was published with the emperor's help, along with the Mass in D minor (with financial assistance from an industrialist, Theodor Haemmerle), the Second Symphony, and Psalm 150. The Eighth Symphony was hailed by audience and critics alike as a great success, with the lonely exception of Hanslick, who wrote of its 'dream-disturbed, cat's misery style'.

Liver and stomach complaints necessitated dieting, which Bruckner hated. In 1893 he was confined to bed for a spell, seriously ill. He wrote to his official biographer, Göllerich, on 10 March: 'I feel totally deserted. Nobody comes to see me, or at least only extremely rarely. The *Wagner-Verein* is everything for them.'

He certainly suffered from loneliness in his last years, yet performances were occurring on a wider and more frequent scale and he still received distinctions such as honorary membership of the *Gesellschaft der Musikfreunde*. The First Symphony was published in 1893, the F minor Mass in 1894, the Fifth Symphony and the E minor Mass in 1896. In 1893 he wrote his last completed work, *Helgoland*, for male chorus and orchestra, first performed on 8 October.

At a performance of the F minor Mass in Vienna in 1893 Brahms applauded so warmly that Bruckner went up to his box to thank him for the gesture. Bruckner made his will, in which he bequeathed the original scores of all his important works, containing his true intentions, to the *Hofbibliothek* in Vienna (now the *Österreichisches National-bibliothek*), 'for later times' as he frequently and significantly remarked. His brother Ignaz and sister Rosalia were named as his heirs. Owing to illness his university lectures were now sporadic and in November 1894 he resigned from the university, thus losing his valued contact with the young. In January of that year he had travelled to Berlin with Hugo Wolf for performances of the Te Deum and Seventh Symphony. Wolf's choruses *Der Feuerreiter* and *Elfenlied* were played at one concert which included the première of a work for chorus and orchestra by Eugen d'Albert. But in April Bruckner was too ill to attend the first performance of his Fifth Symphony under Franz Schalk. This performance was of Schalk's own version, a gross perversion of the dying composer's original intentions.

Bruckner spent his seventieth birthday in Steyr. He received telegrams of congratulation from all over the world, many honorary memberships and the freedom of the city of Linz. By the end of November the first three movements of the Ninth Symphony were complete, and he pressed ahead with his most ambitious finale. His health was now very unsteady and his mind often wandered so far that he was incapable of rational conversation. But to the end he had moments of perfect clarity and never lost interest in completing his symphony, which, as he told his doctor, was to be dedicated 'to the King of Kings, our Lord, and I hope that He will grant me enough time to complete it'. He was unable to climb the stairs to his flat and the emperor put a gatekeeper's lodge at the Schloss Belvedere at his disposal in July 1895.

On 12 January 1896 he attended his last concert—a performance of the Te Deum that had been suggested by none other than Johannes Brahms. He was so ill that he had to be carried into the concert hall to hear a programme that included Wagner's *Das Liebesmahl der Apostel*

Fig. 6 One of the last pages of Bruckner's notebook-diary (29 September—1 October 1896) in which he daily noted, by underlinings, the number of times he said prayers. A = Ave Maria, V = Vater Unser (The Lord's Prayer)

and a new, very advanced symphonic poem, *Till Eulenspiegel*, by Richard Strauss.

The last weeks were clouded by a return of Bruckner's pathological obsessions and there was a hint in his speech of religious mania. Hugo Wolf and Franz Schalk visited him. On Sunday 11 October 1896 he worked on the finale of the Ninth Symphony and in the early afternoon took a walk in the lovely public garden that surrounded the house. Very quietly and without any alarming signs he died on his return. Three days later the *Karlskirche* was thronged by those who came to pay their last respects, and the Adagio of the Seventh Symphony in an arrangement for wind band by Löwe was played. However, two important figures of Bruckner's Vienna years did not enter the church. Hugo Wolf had no ticket and was turned away, and Brahms arrived late, stood at the door, muttered what was thought to be, 'Never mind. Soon my coffin', and left. Bruckner's remains were taken to St Florian, as he had wished, and laid in a splendid sarcophagus exactly beneath the great organ of the *Stiftkirche*.

One of the many remarks attributed to him was his reply prepared for the day when his beloved God would call him to account for the use he had made of his earthly talents: 'I will present to him the score of my Te Deum, and he will judge me mercifully.'

7

Bruckner's character

Bruckner was outwardly a simple man. His music is far from simple. His psychology is not simple to explain. The word 'simple' has too often become a tag attached to him and it is unsatisfactory. It could imply that he was foolish, half-witted, credulous, inexperienced, insignificant, and silly. He was not. He was humble, straightforward, uncomplicated, unpretentious, and unsophisticated in outward manner, and it is in this sense, and this sense only, that he can be described as a simple man. He was warm-hearted and childlike, but his proverbial naïvety should not be confused with a lack of intelligence. His rural background was evident all through his life, yet his great-great-grandfather was the last of his ancestors that can truly be called a peasant. City life never really suited him, and the little countryman, habitually dressed in a somewhat bulky black suit and wide-brimmed black hat, was in sharp contrast to the style and elegance of fashionable Vienna. He never lost his native accent and in his speech was capable at times of rustic bluntness.

Many years of his life were spent in subordinate positions and this undoubtedly affected his social behaviour. His letters are straightforward, and his grammar, style, and handwriting display an educated mind. Yet his many written applications abound with phrases of respect and devotion that border on the obsequious. This was his natural mode of expression, not a deliberately servile attitude but one that originated in the moulding of his character in the years before the social uprisings of 1848. Social forms, customs and usages of the *Vormärz* period were deeply implanted in his mind, and in 1848 itself he was sheltered at St Florian. His thoughts were in another world, and political events did not touch him in the way they did other composers. Furthermore his emergence from this quiet background at an age at which most other composers had made their mark may explain the modest, subservient, and often flowery terms of address he used. He took little interest in the contemporary world, and he was not a 'literary' man in any sense. His library contained at his death only books on music and religion, and two other volumes: one on the Mexican war, and the other on a North Pole expedition. The only occasion on which he considered writing an opera was in 1893, when he studied a libretto by Gertrud Bollé-Hellmund called *Astra* (based on a novel, *Die Toteninsel*, by Richard Voss). He admired the style of this for the significant reasons that it was '*à la Lohengrin*, romantic, full of the mystery of religion, and entirely free from all that is impure'.[1]

In a century when many of the great composers were noted for their artistic letter-writing, and when literature and music were united by strong bonds, Bruckner's lack of literary interest is even more striking. But it does not reflect a lack of education or academic ability. He had distinguished himself in all the examinations for his teaching qualifications and later studied Latin, physics, and law. Fuchs at Windhaag had criticized him for introducing a controversial and forbidden subject in his classes in those pre-1848 years—the elements of Copernican theory. He had a great interest in medical matters and delighted in questioning medical colleagues at the university. Indeed the university circles in which he mixed would not have tolerated him long if he had displayed an untrained mind.

Another result of his youthful environment was his conservative attitude to life. He unquestioningly accepted authority and a social structure of clear class-distinction. His personal life and surroundings were orderly, and he would never have dreamed of flouting convention. Yet he was no prude, and there are many accounts by his pupils of convivial evenings spent in the company of the kindly old man, who had a warm sense of humour and was a lively conversationalist, especially when music was the topic. He was a keen dancer and always attended many balls during the carnival period, until well into his fifties. He had a large appetite for traditional Austrian cooking and enjoyed beer and good wine, but apparently never drank to excess.

Money matters always worried him a great deal but, although he was never rich, he never suffered poverty. He was always careful to see that his finances were secure and was anxious to be insured and certain of an old-age pension. This explains the continual applications for better-paid posts that he made from his St Florian days until the 1880s. He received only one publisher's fee in his life—a mere fifty florins for the Te Deum. Lack of performances seems to have caused him unwarranted anxiety. Every one of his mature works (except the Ninth Symphony) was performed in his lifetime, some of them many times, for example 30 performances of the Te Deum, 23 of the String Quintet, 32 of the Seventh Symphony and 24 of the Third Symphony. This was not a record to become depressed about, but the hostility of the critics and his feeling of financial insecurity led him to complain loud and long about the insignificance of public recognition given to him.

In discussing his uncertainty and lack of self-confidence, a careful distinction must be made between personal matters and musical matters.

[1] Letter to Bollé-Hellmund, 5 September 1893.

He did not lack self-assurance as a composer, and this is borne out by the fact that each new symphony was written before he had heard a performance of the previous one (with the exception of No. 2), and by the short gaps between the completion of one and the beginning of the next, for example two days between Nos. 3 and 4, two months between Nos. 4 and 5, less than three weeks between Nos. 6 and 7, and hardly any gap between the first version of the Eighth and the first sketch for the Ninth. This remarkable display of self-assertion broke down only under extreme pressure (for example after the first performance of the Third Symphony and after Levi's rejection of the Eighth). Nor does lack of self-confidence account for the feverish revising of the last years. It is clear that his work would not have been heard or published to any comparable extent had he not agreed to these new revisions. It was a weak and regrettable action, but quite understandable and expedient for an artist faced with silence. Bruckner had an utter conviction that what he wrote was what he wanted, and carefully preserved his original scores for future generations. The revisions were made under great pressure and also from an urge for perfection, though at a time when his mental condition reduced him to nervous fussiness.

Worldly matters were different, however. He undoubtedly went into more than one panic of uncertainty during his life. With each step in his career he needed the reassurance of friends and patrons that all would be well, otherwise he became confused, indecisive, and incapable of going on. He needed the firmest of ground to tread on, and became obsessed with the collection of testimonials and certificates without which he would have been afraid to proceed in the musical battlefield of Vienna. His long period of study was not the result of a pathological inferiority complex, as has been suggested, but was a necessary stage in his development—an inner compulsion to explore the very essence of music and master every intricacy with infinite patience, without which process his originality might never have been achieved.

It is not necessary to look for historical evidence of Bruckner's belief in himself as a composer. The proof that he knew where he was going, that he discovered his aesthetic and thoroughly mastered it, is in the music itself. And so the strange dichotomy of artist and man reveals itself: Bruckner the man who never lost his Upper Austrian cautiousness, and Bruckner the composer who forged and perfected a conception that was the most significant symphonic step since Beethoven. The facts would suggest that some powerful psychological elements link the provincial organist and the potent symphonic force. A clue may be found in a closer look at his symptoms of nervous disorder, and at his life-long, intense religious fervour.

He frequently oscillated between moods of buoyant optimism and states of depression and despair. The latter were partly the result of distressing professional or emotional experiences, partly inherited (his mother was given to fits of depression), and partly unaccountable, as they occurred even at times of professional success. This temperament, already subject to severe fits of melancholy, was aggravated by a nagging feeling of neglect in the city of the railing Hanslick and the successful Brahms. His three most serious periods of nervous breakdown, which brought him near to insanity, were in 1867, 1887–91, and in the last two years of his life. But for the consolation of his religion and his creative outlet he might well have succumbed to his inner conflicts and obsessions and ended his days in an asylum. Conversely, it may be postulated that but for his inner conflicts he might never have composed.

Manias and obsessions were not confined to periods of crisis. His numeromania is reflected in his scores, both in the meticulous numbering of bars and phrase periods and in obsessive and frenzied repetitions of motifs.[2] He kept a careful list of the number of prayers he said each day, and the number of times he repeated a particular prayer. He also recorded in his diary the number of dances he had with particular girls at a ball. He counted statues during walks in a park and would start all over again if he thought one had been missed. He was obsessed with the need to discover the numbers, characteristics, and substance of inanimate objects, such as the ornamental tops of the municipal towers in Vienna. He had an almost macabre interest in death, or more accurately, in corpses. When Beethoven and Schubert were reinterred in a new burial place, he lost the glass from his pince-nez in his eagerness to catch a glimpse of the remains. He is said to have hurried to the mortuary after a disastrous theatre fire in 1881 to examine the victims' charred bodies, and earlier he had repeatedly requested the Hörsching church authorities to let him have Weiss's skull. In 1868 he wrote to Weinwurm after the assassination of the Emperor Maximilian in Mexico (a country in which he took an intense interest, matched only by the fascination of the severe hardships suffered in a North Pole expedition):

> Even during my illness this was the only thing dear to my heart: Mexico and Maximilian. At all costs I want to see the body of Maximilian. Please, Weinwurm, send someone trustworthy to the palace, or even better make enquiries at the office of the *Oberhofmeister* whether it will be possible to view Maximilian's body, i.e. in an open coffin, or under glass, or whether only the closed coffin will be visible. Then please inform me by telegram so that I do not come too late. I ask you most urgently for this information.

His will contained precise details for the disposal of his remains, and it seems fitting that his sarcophagus lies in the crypt of St Florian surrounded by piles of skulls and bones of long-departed brothers of the foundation.

His relations with women, or rather with a succession of young girls, were unsuccessful and unhappy, but do not appear to have seriously dis-

---

[2] Schumann had a similar obsession with certain rhythmic constructions.

turbed his life or work, although he permanently longed for the security of marriage. In his diary he recorded the names of all the girls who had attracted him, and on his holiday in 1880 the list becomes quite long. He was rejected with unfailing frequency and yet he was never daunted. He wrote in a letter of November 1885: 'As for my getting married, I have no bride as yet. If only I could find a really suitable, dear girl!' But all the winsome teenagers he approached found him unattractive and rarely took his offers of marriage with any seriousness.

His life-long and deepest love, that for his 'dear God', affords the most important insight into his personality. His was no Pauline conversion, but an inborn, steadfast and undying faith. He lived in two worlds, the everyday one and the world of his meditations, in which, as Hans-Hubert Schönzeler has written,[3] 'he may have attained visionary realms which found their expression in his music'. For him God and the world of transcendent spirit were realities which he never questioned. From the quiet, firm state of grace which he was able to reach came both calm in his distress and renewed strength for creative work. It is recorded that he always prayed deeply before improvising and that in lessons his pupils would become aware that his attention was no longer with them. The Angelus was ringing, and he was praying. A mystic in an unmystical age, the thoughts of the spirit that filled him were the life-spring of his art.

[3] *Bruckner* (London, 1970; rev. edn, 1978).

8

Critics and interpreters

The nineteenth century saw the childhood and adolescence of musical criticism. By the time of Bruckner's creative maturity it had all the worst characteristics of an early manhood: rashness, intolerance, and ambition for power. In Vienna this was especially evident because the musical world was firmly divided between the partisans of Brahms and Wagner respectively. The effect of critical hostility on Bruckner's composing activities was not particularly marked. It was almost always the opinions and advice of his friends that led to his periods of creative distress, revising, and dearth of original composition. But his personal life was tormented by the critics who railed at him; it made him nervous about performing or publishing his music in the way he had written it, and many of his letters reveal the misery and anguish he suffered at the hands of Hanslick and his adherents, who saw him as a bungling Simple Simon, writing Wagnerian works of chronic prolixity.

Even allowing for the extreme lengths to which a reviewer might go in those years of gleeful mud-slinging, it is difficult to be charitable towards Hanslick, who was in a position of such giddy power that he could make a statement such as: 'When I wish to annihilate, then I do annihilate.' Tovey, a friend of Joachim and an enthusiastic advocate of Brahms, summed up Bruckner's grimmest enemy admirably:

> Hanslick . . . saw in Bruckner fair game. Wagner gave Hanslick only too lenient a treatment when he immortalised him in Beckmesser, named Hans Lich in the first sketch of the poem of *Meistersinger*. Beckmesser at all events knew the rules he so humbly adored. I have read Hanslick's collected works patiently without discovering either in his patronage of Brahms or in his attacks on Wagner, Verdi, Bruckner, the early works of Beethoven, Palestrina's *Stabat Mater*, or any other work a little off the average Viennese concert-goer's track in 1880, any knowledge of anything whatever. The general and musical culture shown in Hanslick's writings represents one of the unlovelier forms of parasitism; that which, having the wealth to collect *objets d'art* and the birth and education to talk amusingly, does not itself attempt a stroke of artistic work, does not dream of revising a first impression, experiences the fine arts entirely as the pleasures of a gentleman, and then pronounces judgment as if the expression of its opinion were a benefit and a duty to society.[1]

[1] *Essays in Musical Analysis*, vol. 2 (Oxford, 1935); new edn, 1981, vol. entitled *Symphonies and other Orchestral Works*, p. 254.

1. Bruckner in 1854

2. Interior of the church, St Florian

3. Bruckner in 1868

4. Linz in Bruckner's time

5. A page of the manuscript of the 'Wagner' Symphony No. 3, Adagio

6. A page of the sketch for the Finale of Symphony No. 5

7. A page of the manuscript of the Finale of Symphony No. 7. Note the bar-period numberings in this and in plate 6

8. Bruckner, about 1890

9. Bruckner on a journey in 1885; he loved trains, which held great fascination for him. Caricature by Grandi

10. Bruckner at his Bösendorfer, about 1894

Hanslick's criticism is not just damning, it is glossed over with smooth sarcasm and fatuous insincerity:

> We have no wish to hurt this composer for whom we entertain a high regard both as man and artist and whose musical aims are sincere, albeit their treatment is strange.
>
> Like every one of Bruckner's works, the E major symphony contains ingenious inspirations, interesting and even pleasant details—here six, there eight bars—but in between the lightnings there are interminable stretches of darkness, leaden boredom and feverish over-excitement.[2]

And on the Eighth Symphony:

> A characteristic is the abrupt juxtaposition of dry contrapuntal schoolroom-style and immoderate exaltation. Thus, flung about hither and thither between drunkenness and dreariness, we reach no definite impression, enjoy no artistic pleasure. Everything flows, without clarity, without order, willy-nilly into a cruel long-windedness.[3]

When in 1884 Anton Vergeiner of Freistadt informed Bruckner that he intended to write an article about him in a paper, the composer wrote: 'Please do not write anything against Hanslick for my sake. His fury is dreadful. He is in a position to annihilate other people. With him one cannot fight. One can only approach him with petitions, but even that is of no use to me, because to me he is never at home.' At the end of a letter to Nikisch of 23 November 1888, he wrote, 'Hanslick!!! Bülow!!! Joachim!!! For God's sake! I work as much as possible!'

Bruckner's protagonists were able to get their own back from time to time, and in no less forceful language. Hugo Wolf declared that 'one single cymbal crash by Bruckner is worth all the four symphonies of Brahms with the serenades thrown in'. A number of musical journals and the critics Ludwig Speidel and Theodor Helm championed Bruckner, especially in the last fifteen years of his life. But, to turn aside from polemics, it is not hard to appreciate that vast sections of the musical public, reared on the Viennese classics and Mendelssohn, Schumann, and Brahms, could not grasp the huge symphonic statements that Bruckner patiently unfolded. These works shattered previously held conceptions and therefore made slow progress, especially outside German-speaking countries.

Two men who had ruffled Bruckner's creative calm later became converts. Bülow, who wrote many sarcastic references to him in his letters and declared in 1888 that his symphonies were 'the anti-musical ravings of a half-wit', relented in 1891 when he called the Te Deum a splendid work, worthy of public performance. In 1877 Bruckner called Hans Richter 'the generalissimo of deceit'. Richter tried to have the best of both worlds in Vienna and was at that time giving the first performances

---

[2] *Neue Freie Presse*, March 1886.   [3] Ibid., December 1892.

of the Brahms symphonies. He was on occasions insincere to Bruckner but in later years, when the tide had turned in Bruckner's favour and Brahms's symphonic output was exhausted, he gave a great many performances of his works. Other notable conductors of Bruckner's works during his lifetime included his own pupils Löwe, Mottl, Nikisch, and the Schalk brothers; also Herbeck, Wilhelm Jahn, Karl Muck, Levi, Siegfried Ochs, and Anton Seidl.

Mahler's piano-duet arrangement of the Third Symphony delighted Bruckner, who presented him with the manuscript score of the work. Mahler was a keen if discriminating admirer of Bruckner, he was always a welcome visitor at Bruckner's flat, and the two men corresponded when Mahler moved to Hamburg in 1893. After Bruckner's death Mahler continued to champion him, performing the Symphonies 4, 5, and 6 in Vienna from 1899 to 1901, and all the symphonies in New York in 1908. Although his attitude towards Bruckner, and also to Hugo Wolf and Richard Strauss, became more critical in his later years, he made an arrangement with Universal Edition in 1910 that all royalties on his works should go towards publication of and propaganda for Bruckner's music.

Bruckner criticism in the early years of this century took some time to shake off 'the ghost of old Klingsor', Wagner, whose influence on Bruckner's style was exaggerated in books such as that of Rudolf Louis (Munich, 1905). Max Auer wrote a book in angry response to this but it did not appear in print until 1923. August Göllerich, the official biographer, who was responsible for many performances of Bruckner's music, including the lesser-known works, died in 1923 having completed only a few chapters and some sketches. Auer then saw the long four-volume study through the press and it was completed in 1936. The conductor Franz Moissl stimulated interest in Bruckner's early orchestral development with performances of the Overture in G minor, and the Symphonies No. 0 and in F minor between 1921 and 1924. At this time increasing enthusiasm for Bruckner had led to the formation of a Vienna Bruckner League, which was the nucleus for an International Bruckner League (1925), and in turn resulted in the foundation of the International Bruckner Society (*Internationalen Bruckner-Gesellschaft*) in 1929. Meanwhile the books of Decsey, Orel, Kurth, and Halm lifted the Wagnerian veil, and the popularization of Bruckner (hampered by the lack of 'saleable' works such as songs or piano pieces) was under way on an international scale.

This process was helped by the appearance from the early 1930s of Bruckner's scores in their 'original' versions (which will be considered in the following chapter) and by the continuing succession of fine interpreters: Felix Weingartner, Bruno Walter, Carl Schuricht, Otto Klemperer, Wilhelm Furtwängler, Jascha Horenstein, Hans Knappertsbusch, and (with the Royal Concertgebouw Orchestra) Edouard van Beinum.

Siegmund von Hausegger, conductor of the Munich Philharmonic, gave a concert on 2 April 1932 at which the Ninth Symphony was played twice: first in the then familiar but spuriously Wagnerian score by Löwe, and secondly in the version as prepared for the New Complete Edition by Robert Haas. Hausegger went on to première the Haas editions of Symphony No. 5 (28 October 1935) and No. 4 (16 November 1936). It is grimly ironic that in the view of many, such as the arch-conservative and Nazi enthusiast Hausegger, this renaissance of Bruckner's work was an aspect of the rebirth of the German spirit under the aegis of the Third Reich. On 6 June 1937 Adolf Hitler unveiled and laid a wreath at a bust of Bruckner in the Walhalla near Regensburg during a festival of the International Bruckner Society. There is famous propaganda newsreel footage of this event, at which Hausegger conducted the Adagio from the Eighth Symphony.

Hitler, like Bruckner, was born in Upper Austria and educated in Linz. He professed enormous admiration for Bruckner and, after the *Anschluss* of 1938, made funds available from his personal coffers for the furtherance of Bruckner editions and performances. He envisaged Linz as the new cultural capital of the Reich and St Florian as a second Bayreuth. The Nazis viewed Bruckner as an ideal son of the *Volk*: an artist who rose from racially pure peasant stock to celebrate the Teutonic strength and spirit in bold, romantic, yet also austere grandiloquence, perhaps the ideal of Goebbels's vision of a 'romanticism of steel'. The National Socialist Reichs Symphony Orchestra played at both huge party rallies and in village halls: Bruckner's Fourth Symphony was a standard of their repertory, and according to Erwin Bauer was perceived as a 'hymn of love for the German homeland'.[4] Hitler's hope of a Bruckner Orchestra in Linz was realized in the season 1943–4 with the creation of the national touring and broadcasting *Bruckner-Orchester St Florian des Gross-Deutschen Rundfunks*. In these dark years of war several other important Bruckner interpreters made their mark in the Reich: Joseph Keilberth, Oswald Kabasta (who succeeded Hausegger as conductor of the Munich Philharmonic in 1938 and who committed suicide early in 1946, compromised by his strong association with the Austrian Nazis), Eugen Jochum, Karl Böhm, and Herbert von Karajan.

Empires collapse in ruins; music lives on. The effect of the Nazi appropriation of Bruckner (as with their glorification of the 'Aryan' Bach and Handel) was significant for the effect it had upon the all-important matter of the editions of the scores themselves, as will be shown shortly.

It could be argued that the emphasis on Teutonic monumentality and romantic grandeur in Bruckner's scores served only to slow further his crossing of international frontiers. In the long term his universality has

---

[4] Quoted in Erik Levi, *Music in the Third Reich* (London, 1994).

been triumphantly vindicated thanks to the achievement of another generation or two of devoted and deeply intuitive conductors and scholars. In the USA the journal of the Bruckner Society of America, *Chord and Discord*, reflects this, as do the writings of the sane and wise English enthusiasts Deryck Cooke and Robert Simpson. The post-war period has benefitted from interpreters of distinction such as Bernard Haitinck (who, like Jochum, recorded an early cycle of all the symphonies with the Concertgebouw Orchestra), Karajan's later work with the Berlin Philharmonic (which reveals fascinating differences in approach over the decades), Daniel Barenboim's performance with the same orchestra, and the recordings, live and in studio, of Franz Welser-Möst, Kurt Sanderling, Klaus Tennstedt, Carlo Maria Giulini, Eliahu Inbal, and Günter Wand.

Another significant development of recent times has been the application of 'authentic' performance practice to this late-nineteenth-century composer. This entails not just the playing of the works on instruments using the materials, pitch, and component parts of those of the date of Bruckner's first performances, but also applying interpretative details such as phrasing, intonation, etc. Enthusiasts such as Roger Norrington, and several others, have brought a surprisingly fresh approach to the orchestral and choral-instrumental works in this way.

Finally, in the publications since 1979 of the Anton Bruckner-Institut Linz, under the principal editorship first of Franz Grasberger and latterly Othmar Wessely, a vast amount of material relating to critical reception and aspects of interpretation (as well as new biographical information) has been presented, notably in the series of *Bruckner Yearbooks*, the volumes entitled *Dokumente und Studien* and the *Bruckner-Symposiumsberichte* (details are given in Appendix D).

9

The problem of revisions

In determining which versions of Bruckner's works represent the composer's true intentions a complicated and confusing series of problems arises, not equalled in the case of any other composer. The purpose of this chapter is to unfold as clearly and simply as is possible the history of the various revisions, versions, and editions, without exploring the ramifications of each individual text—a task that would be beyond the scope of this book.[1]

Bruckner was a perfectionist when it came to his scores, which are clear and precise in layout. It was natural for him to revise a work more than once after completing it and he did so habitually from his first to his last creative years. It is not revisions such as these that present the problem. Johann Herbeck, after mighty efforts, succeeded in persuading him to make considerable alterations to the Third Symphony for its 1876 performance. Joseph Schalk and Ferdinand Löwe then persuaded him to agree to changes in orchestration and other details in the Seventh Symphony in 1883. But the most disastrous period of revision occurred after Levi's rejection of the Eighth Symphony in 1887. Joseph Schalk aided Bruckner in the revision of the work, and Franz Schalk assisted in the final recomposition of the Third. It should be clearly stated that the Schalk brothers, Löwe, and others who aided Bruckner did so out of a genuine wish to further the composer's recognition and his chances of performance and publication. To this end they worked devotedly for many years. The tragedy lies in the fact that these friends were pronounced Wagnerians, and while they loved Bruckner's music, they seriously misunderstood his language and mode of expression. However, Bruckner's rather malleable attitude to his friends' suggestions was seen by them as the indication of a free hand to bring out their own editions in print. In the process of this they transformed Brucknerian economy

[1] Deryck Cooke's series of articles *The Bruckner Problem Simplified* (see Bibliography) summed up the situation admirably in 1969. Since then several new editions have appeared which alter the position he adopted with regard to some works. For the reader of German there are also the papers of the 1980 Bruckner-Symposium in Linz, *Die Fassungen*, ed. Franz Grasberger, 1981. The prefaces (in German and English) to each volume of the *Anton Bruckner Kritische Gesamtausgabe* (Complete Edition, 1951–) are invaluable.

of scoring into Wagnerian luxury. They cut out portions, and freely altered tempo and expression marks, barring, dynamics, and phrasing. Indeed the worst excesses, such as Franz Schalk's edition (1896) of the Fifth Symphony and Löwe's edition (1903) of the Ninth, involved the actual recomposition of extended passages.

Bruckner naturally protested about much of this but no one listened to him. To no avail he wrote letters begging that whatever might happen in performance, his published scores should not be altered, and he refused to give the approval of his signature to the Schalk-Löwe version of the Fourth Symphony. As Table 1 shows, there were no less than twenty-six different possibilities of Bruckner's nine symphonies in existence, including his own original versions and revisions, and the scores of his friends. Of the ten published works that this table lists, not one score represented the composer's real thoughts.

Fortunately Bruckner's manuscripts were entrusted by the terms of his last will to the care of the Austrian National Library in Vienna. By the late 1920s there were insistent calls for something to be done about the

Table 1. Symphonies 1–9: completion dates of each version and dates of publication up to 1903[1]

No.	Version	Publication
1	1866	
	1891	1893
2	1872	
	1877	
	1892	1892
3	1873	
	1877	1878
	1889	
	1890	1890
4	1874	
	1880	
		1889
5	1876	1896
6	1881	1899
7	1883	1885
8	1887	
	1890	1892
9[2]	1894	1903

[1] For greater details of chronology and editions, see Appendix B.
[2] First three movements.

urgent need for an authentic complete edition. So, over thirty-two years after the composer's death, the International Bruckner Society, under the presidency of Max Auer, met for the first time on 17 February 1929. Their pre-eminent task was the publication of his works in their original form. Scores of the Requiem and the Missa Solemnis were the first to appear in the early 1930s. The plan to replace the spurious editions of the symphonies and issue new critical scores at first met not only with scepticism but with hostility, and with the strong opposition of Franz Schalk. In 1932, however, a year after Schalk's death, Hausegger's performance of both versions of the Ninth Symphony in the same concert overcame almost all doubts, and the International Bruckner Society created the *Musikwissenschaftlicher Verlag*, expressly to fulfil their ideal, with Robert Haas as scientific director of the new edition, assisted by Alfred Orel. Leopold Nowak joined the team in 1937. The following works were issued between 1934 and 1944:

Four Orchestral Pieces (1862) Orel, 1934

Overture in G minor (1862) Orel, 1934

Symphony No. 1 (1866 'Linz' version) Haas, 1935

                (1891 'Vienna' version) Haas, 1935

    No. 2 (in a hybrid score of the 1872 and 1877 versions) Haas, 1938

    No. 4 (1880 version) Haas, 1936

    No. 5 Haas, 1935

    No. 6 Haas, 1935

    No. 7 Haas, 1944

    No. 8 (in a hybrid score of the 1887 and 1890 versions) Haas, 1939

    No. 9 Orel, 1934

Mass in E minor (1882 version) Haas and Nowak, 1940

Mass in F minor Haas, 1944

During these years, and especially following the *Anschluss* of 1938, the Nazi government seized the opportunity to use the International Bruckner Society as an unwitting tool for their propaganda. Hitler gave money personally to promote their work of publication. This seriously harmed the Society's reputation and damaged its international credibility. In 1945 the complete stock of the publishers was destroyed in a bombing raid on Leipzig. At the end of the war Robert Haas was replaced as editor by Leopold Nowak.

From 1951 Nowak brought out an entirely new set of all the symphonies,[2] chamber music, and major choral works, in fact a New

[2] Except for the later revision of Symphony No. 1 (1891) which was edited by Günter Brosche, director of the music department of the Austrian National Library; and Psalm 150, edited by Franz Grasberger. The shorter sacred choral works were edited by Nowak in collaboration with Hans Bauernfeind; and the various St Florian cantatas, together with *Germanenzug* and *Helgoland* in collaboration with Franz Burkhart and Rudolf Führer.

Complete Bruckner Edition, and in many cases his editorial view conflicted with that of Haas. Nowak died in 1991. The outline shape of the Complete Edition[3] he had brought almost to complete fruition is shown in Table 2. Editions in preparation at the time of writing are shown in Table 3.

Table 2

Volume	
1–9	Symphonies 1–9
10	Symphony in F minor
11	Symphony No. '0'
12/1	Rondo for String Quartet
12/2–3	Piano Works (ed. Walburga Litschauer)
12/4–5	Early Orchestral Works (ed. Hans Jancik and Rüdiger Bornhöft)
12/7	*Abendklänge*, Violin and Piano (ed. Litschauer)
13/1	String Quartet
13/2	String Quintet and Intermezzo
14	Requiem
15	Missa Solemnis
16	Mass in D minor
17	Mass in E minor (two versions)
18	Mass in F minor
19	Te Deum
21	Short Church Music Works (the motets and small-scale Masses)
22	Cantatas and Choral Works (including *Helgoland*)

Table 3

Volume	
2/1	Symphony No. 2, first version of 1872 (ed. William Carragan)
12/6	Organ Works (ed. Erwin Horn)
12/8	March in E flat for Military Band (ed. Bornhöft)
20	Psalms and Magnificat (ed. Paul Hawkshaw)
23/1	Songs (ed. Litschauer)
23/2	Choruses (ed. Carragan)

The devoted work of Haas and Nowak has brought the symphonies of Anton Bruckner to the public in a form closer to his intentions than would have seemed possible in the early years of this century. Both editors carried out their tasks with irreproachable integrity. But the broad question remains for the general listener, Haas or Nowak? The editions of Haas are thoroughly Brucknerian in spirit and he admirably fulfilled

---

[3] Edited by Nowak unless otherwise stated.

his intention of providing performing versions of high artistic worth. In his so-called hybrid scores, those of Symphonies No. 2 and No. 8, his conflation of texts is designed to achieve a thoroughly effective structural result, although scholars will no doubt endlessly debate the merits of such an approach. Nowak's attitude was undoubtedly the more scientific and has resulted in an edition distinguished by the highest qualities of musicology.

What are the most important divergencies between Haas and Nowak? With a number of Bruckner's larger works there is self-evidently no problem to consider, where only Nowak's edition (representing Bruckner's own intentions) exists: the Mass in D minor, the Te Deum, Psalm 150, and the String Quintet and Intermezzo. In the cases of Symphonies No. 1 (both versions), No. 5, No. 6, and No. 9, the final version of the E minor Mass, and the Requiem, Nowak's editions are virtually identical to those of Haas, and are mainly concerned with correcting small errors and oversights. With the F minor Mass, Nowak incorporated new material which had recently come to light. The contentious cases therefore remain Symphonies 2, 3, 4, 7, and 8.

The Second Symphony exists in three versions: the definitive original score of 1872; Bruckner's revision of 1877; and a final re-working of 1892. The last was not a whole-scale re-working and he largely confined himself to altering expression and tempo markings, apart from suggesting a drastic cut in the finale. The 1892 version was undoubtedly influenced by 'friends' with a view to its publication that year, and so may be set aside. The earlier revisions of 1876–7 were begun for a performance arranged by Herbeck but conducted by Bruckner in February 1876. Herbeck had persuaded Bruckner to make a number of cuts and Robert Haas suggested that out of respect for his dear friend and champion (who had died in October) Bruckner allowed the version to stand. He did not, however, destroy the 1872 score. Haas therefore restored the cuts in his hybrid score. Nowak printed the 1877 version as Bruckner left it. In this case I feel that, on the whole, the Haas score is the more effective; but the question will be clarified when the (as yet unpublished) 1872 original score appears in the Complete Edition.

The Third Symphony presents the most complex case of all. It is not, however, a matter here of Haas *versus* Nowak, for Haas never edited No. 3. In truth, there is no satisfactory version of it. There are three full versions by the composer himself (1873, 1877, and 1889), a separate version of the Adagio dating from 1876, two published scores in Bruckner's lifetime which both contain further differences, plus a myriad of minor alterations between all of these. When I first wrote this chapter in the early 1970s the most satisfactory score seemed to be that of the 1877 version as edited by Fritz Oeser in 1950. This had long seemed preferable to the Bruckner-Schalk score of 1889 which Nowak re-issued in 1959. The 1889 version contains a number of recomposed, re-orchestrated passages, the effect of which is to graft the more complex style of his later years onto the simpler style of the early 1870s. It is severely cut and again the influence of friends is strongly evident. Then, in 1977, Nowak issued the 1873 score, Bruckner's authentic first thoughts without any cuts or modifications (other than a few genuine improvements made in 1874). The effect of this publication was revelatory. Although by no means a perfect piece of musical architecture, this first version of the 'Wagner' Symphony contains so much of what Bruckner had been striving to achieve in his previous scores that it instantly demonstrated how all his subsequent attempts to improve it were misguided. The reasons why Bruckner himself did not see this are extremely complicated and go beyond the mere influence of friends. What matters is that in the Nowak 1873 score we have the first version of this crucial milestone in his epic symphonic march. Nowak subsequently issued a fine edition of the 1877 version (1981) and of the intermediate 1876 Adagio (1980).

The Fourth Symphony also exists in three versions but the last of these, overwhelmingly the effort of Löwe and Joseph Schalk (although supervised by Bruckner), may be set aside. The earlier history of this piece is nearly as complex as that of No. 3, and the Fourth underwent even more drastic metamorphosis. Its first version of 1874 is confident, if over-comfortably spacious. In 1878 an entirely new 'Hunt' Scherzo was added, and the finale was radically rewritten and abridged. In 1880 the finale was again newly composed. Haas issued the 1878 score with the 'Hunt' Scherzo and the 1880 finale (this 1936 score contains the 1878 finale as an appendix). Nowak issued (for the first time) the original 1874 score (1975), the 1878 finale (1981), and in his edition (1953) of the 1878–80 second version (with 'Hunt' Scherzo and 1880 finale) he also incorporated further material from 1886 which had recently come to light in New York.

In the Seventh Symphony Nowak includes orchestral alterations that Bruckner made for the first performance by Nikisch. These do not matter very much, but it seems unfortunate that Nikisch's 'conductor's markings' (approved by Bruckner for the same performance) were also retained, as they can interrupt the flow of the music unless the conductor takes great care.

The Eighth Symphony presents a picture of a different kind. Haas incorporated elements of the 1887 version in his edition of the 1890 score, in a conjectural attempt to remove the influence of Joseph Schalk. The result is eminently Brucknerian and a very satisfying piece of creative editing. Nowak, true to his scientific approach, has issued the 1887 and 1890 versions separately. In my view the Haas edition has a structural balance, breadth, and grandeur that seem ideal in performance, yet Nowak's edition of the tauter 1890 revision has received some eloquent interpretations.

10

Conception of Mass and symphony

Bruckner was born in a Romantic age and, it has often and quite rightly been remarked, that is almost all he had in common with it. Both his outward personality and his musical style are out of keeping with the typical image of the nineteenth-century composer. He seems rather to embody the habits and manner, if not exactly the style, of a Baroque or even late Renaissance master. His immense contrapuntal skill, his virtuosity at the organ, his ability to incorporate archaic forms in his own forward-looking idiom, and his devotion to Sechter's theories are all reflections of this. He was attracted to music of the Baroque era, and his love for it is echoed in the primitive lustre of his brass writing, the boldness and width of his designs, and the naïve joy in polyphony that is magnificently conveyed in all the larger mature sacred works and which finds its symphonic culmination in the finale of Symphony No. 5. The rich splendour of his symphonic brass writing is clearly a development of his early predilection for brass instrumentation. Something of the magnificence of antiphonal brass writing associated with St Mark's Cathedral in Venice in the Renaissance era lives on in Bruckner's early music, for example in the unfinished *Missa pro Quadragesima* of 1846, the Requiem (1849), the Cantata *Auf Brüder, auf, zur frohen Feier* (1852, with 2 trumpets, 3 horns, and bass trombone), Psalm 114 (1852, with 3 trombones), *Vor Arneths Grab* (1854, with 3 trombones), and the 'Libera' in F minor (1854, also with trombones). There are also two remarkable short, chorale-like and richly harmonized movements for trombones alone, *Aequale*, of 1847 (written in memory of his godmother, Rosalie Mayrhofer).

The three great Mass settings in D minor, E minor, and F minor of the 1860s encompass the first period of Bruckner's creative maturity. Those in D minor and F minor are symphonic Masses in the tradition of Beethoven's Missa Solemnis and Cherubini's Requiem Masses. The predominant influence upon them is the Viennese classical Mass as perfected by Haydn and Mozart, and developed further in different ways by Cherubini, Schubert, and Beethoven, but the baroque element is never far from sight. The combined influence of Bach, the Viennese classical composers, and the dramatic Mass style of Beethoven gives Bruckner's

Masses a depth of devotional character not paralleled in the sacred works of his contemporaries. There is no evidence that the sacred works of Liszt influenced Bruckner at this or any other time (although this has been suggested), but the two men shared an interest in plainsong which is strongly evident in each of Bruckner's Masses and pervades many sacred works of Liszt.

The essential feature of the Masses in D minor and F minor is the symphonic element, which in both works fuses the various contrasting sections of the Mass into one unified whole. This is not achieved at the expense of harmonic and melodic enhancement of individual sections of the text. Instead the symphonic conception creates unity in diversity. The orchestra plays an important role in the overall texture and often has themes of its own which are developed in truly symphonic style. One of the predominant features of Bruckner's symphonies is the thematic linking of the outer movements, and frequently the main theme of the opening movement returns in a triumphant statement in the last bars of the finale. This has its roots in these Masses, where there are reminiscences of the Kyrie in the 'Dona nobis pacem'—a traditional feature of Mass composition. In the Agnus Dei of the Mass in D minor the first Kyrie theme appears both at the opening and at the close, scale motifs which pervade much of the Mass are strongly evident, and the 'miserere' theme from the Gloria, the 'Amen' fugue subject of the Gloria, and the 'Et vitam venturi' theme from the Credo are quoted. In this procedure lie the seeds of the quotations in the finales of Symphonies 3, 4, 5, and 8. The use of fugue to heighten tension towards the end of Symphony No. 5 and the String Quintet may also stem from the final sections of the Glorias of all three Masses and the Credo of the F minor Mass.

Specific fingerprints of Bruckner's later symphonic style can also be pointed out in the Masses. The endings of the Gloria and Credo in both the D minor and F minor Masses have a definite feeling of the close of a symphonic movement. The Hosanna of the Benedictus of the D minor Mass has an exuberant yet characteristically abrupt close followed by a rest. This effect is used several times in the Masses and is designed to exploit fully a fine cathedral acoustic. Similar moments in the symphonies (such as the pauses after the mighty brass chords near the opening of Symphony No. 5) show that Bruckner had the same resonant acoustic effect in mind. Many harmonic and melodic features of the Masses, such as step-wise, parallel movements of parts in a climax, pedal points, a fondness for leaps of the sixth and octave and broad statements of the full tonic major, are personal characteristics of the composer that abound in his symphonies. The most obvious link between Mass and symphony is found in the many quotations from these three great Masses in the Symphonies 0, 2, 3 and 9. These and other 'cross-quotations' are another feature of Bruckner's style which will be discussed in their proper place.

When Bruckner turned from symphonic Mass to monumental symphony he was making no concession to popular mid-nineteenth-century taste. Both had long been declining in fashion. Wagner had declared that the symphonic conception of Beethoven's Ninth and the great Schubert C major was extinct. The symphonies of Berlioz and Liszt were vast canvases of programme music, and those of Mendelssohn and Schumann were confined both within the symphonic limitations of those composers and within the bounds of the Romantic lyrical world they explored. Brahms had so far written none, but by the time Bruckner made his first real impression on the musical world (i.e. in the mid-1880s) Brahms was fully successful and established. Bruckner's very originality dispenses with the necessity to comment further on his relationship to any of these men, with the exceptions of Schubert (with whom he had a number of stylistic affinities which will shortly be discussed) and Beethoven, who provides a starting point for Bruckner in one particular work, namely the Choral Symphony. However, Beethoven's Ninth was not a model that Bruckner copied in an automatic way. It was instead a dramatic discovery which filled out his stream of thought and after which he shaped his own path with renewed individuality. He learned from it, but never imitated it so slavishly as has sometimes been stated. It may have suggested to him a mould, but what filled the mould was as far removed from the original as late Beethoven was from early Haydn.

The most serious charge laid against Bruckner's symphonic conception is that it is 'formless'. This is a justified comment if levelled against the first published versions, which, with their many transformations and cuts, fully deserve such a verdict. But to label the original versions of these works 'formless' is clearly a proof of Dryden's wisdom: 'By education most have been misled: So they believe, because they were so bred.' The lazy musical analyst, eyes open only to the truths of sonata form, can cope with Beethoven and Brahms. Faced with the obstacle of Bruckner in his path, he can only excuse his shortsightedness and impatience by pronouncing the works 'formless'. Certainly Bruckner struggled with problems of form and did not entirely overcome them until he wrote Symphony No. 5 (his seventh symphonic work). This was not the result of a misunderstanding of Classical sonata form, but a slow yet Herculean unfolding of his own originality. He could not build his city in a day, nor could he have built it at all had his slow unfolding been the result of mere ineptitude in coping with basic construction. We do not dismiss *Othello* because of the demerits of *Titus Andronicus*.

With each Bruckner symphony there is an intensification of vision. Again the lazy analyst will conclude that they are all much the same, rather like plaster-cast models differentiated only by a few outward transformations—the work of an impoverished artist with a mania for repetition. Again this conclusion is the voice of a critic, obviously deaf but not, unfortunately, dumb, who cannot comprehend a creative development that does not follow the clear, step-wise logic of Beethoven's pattern. Bruckner had only one symphonic conception and this was developed organically, overcoming problems with each new work in a more complete and satisfactory way, and unfolding new ideas which would flower in his next symphony. Symphonies 1, 0, and 2 are the first stage in this process of organic development. Symphony No. 3 uncovers the most important roots of Bruckner's style, and this and Symphony No. 4 gave him more work and involved more revision than any others. But they are not apprentice works, and their achievements belittle their weaknesses. They are products from a master's forge and he perfected his mould in Symphony No. 5, after which any kind of clear sub-division, as is possible in discussing Beethoven's creative periods, cannot be attempted.

Fingerprints of style and general comments on the overall shape of Bruckner's symphonic conception can be formulated, however. Of the four elements—rhythm, melody, harmony, and orchestration—the last two are often cited as Wagnerian in derivation. Bruckner's orchestration is economic and frequently austere. The orchestra called for in Symphonies 1, 0, and 2 is double woodwind, 4 horns, 2 trumpets 3 trombones, 2 timpani, and strings. Symphony No. 3 adds an extra trumpet, No. 4 adds one tuba, and Nos. 5 and 6 call for 3 timpani. Only Symphonies 7, 8, and 9 involve triple woodwind (but without piccolo), 8 horns and 4 Wagner tubas. The Adagio of Symphony No. 8 includes harps (3 if possible), and 'exotic' percussion effects are confined to two cymbal and triangle crashes (there is also one at exactly the same point in the Adagio of Symphony No. 7 which is of questionable authenticity). The orchestral sound is never Wagnerian and there is the conspicuous absence in the modest forces listed above of Wagner's beloved bass clarinet and cor anglais. Wagner's orchestration is smoothly resonant and rich in instrumental colour effects. Bruckner, even when employing his fullest brass ensemble, is economical in his use of massed effects, and his orchestral technique relies more on a clear linear style than on the building-up of colour. His orchestration is built up in terraces reminiscent of an organist moving from one manual to another and adding new voices to highlight a line in his tapestry. It is hard and ascetic and clearly emphasizes the thematic sectionalization of the music in a way quite alien to the rich homogeneity and frequent lavishness of Wagner. Nor did Bruckner imitate *Tristan*. His harmony is as bold as Wagner's, even at points in the Mass in D minor (of pre-*Tristan* date), but is never reminiscent of him; and that he could be bolder than Wagner is well illustrated in Symphony No. 9, especially in the opening theme of the Adagio (Ex. 1). Wagner was clearly not Bruckner's model either in orchestration or in harmony. But he certainly learned from Wagner a number of techniques which found expression within the framework of his individual language. Among these are the profoundly emotional espressivo quali-

Ex. 1

ties of the string writing in his Adagios, the strong, arresting effect of pronounced brass entries and the concept of building up long harmonic paragraphs. These are general features common to the works of both men and yet they find expression in very different voices and contexts. To point to an overtly Wagnerian bar in a Bruckner symphony is thus a difficult task: perhaps only the odd appoggiatura or turn of phrase is left to suggest Bayreuth. The opening themes of Bruckner's symphonies from No. 3 onwards do have a leitmotif quality, but it requires a tortuous stretching of definitions to equate their subsequent development with Wagnerian technique.

Bruckner uses a characteristic rhythm, ♩ ♩ ♩ ♩ ♩ or ♩ ♩ ♩ ♩ ♩, with such frequency from Symphony No. 2 (where it appears in dotted rhythm) onwards, that it has become known as 'the Bruckner rhythm'. This rhythmic pattern could well have its origin in the frequent two-four and three-four bar sequences of the Upper Austrian folk music he knew so well.

Syncopation is another rhythmic device that adds variety to a number of passages and enhances their forward motion, for example the 'Et incarnatus est' and 'Crucifixus' sections of the Mass in F minor, the Adagio of Symphony No. 3 (before letter C) and the first movement of Symphony No. 5 (letter F). Even more characteristic is Bruckner's fondness for starting a theme with a rest at the beginning of the bar, for example the opening theme of the Adagio of Symphony No. 6, the 'second theme' of the first movement of No. 4, the 'second themes' of the Adagios of Nos. 7 and 9, the first finale theme of No. 7, and in many other instances.[1]

[1] See music examples 26, 29, and 30.

Wide melodic spans and dramatic leaps are common. Example 2 shows the 'third theme' from the First Symphony's opening movement (in its 1891 version).

Ex. 2

Bruckner's phrase-lengths are predominantly of four and eight bars. In his weaker moments these can become unrelentingly tedious (a weakness not unique among Teutonic composers), but this is in most cases avoided by the richness and variety of detail that his phrase-groups contain. The harmonic content and the 'rhythm' in which the harmony moves help to redeem the regularity of the phrase-lengths. Four-bar phrases are part of Bruckner's language and they are tiny units in the massive span of his slowly unfolding movements. There is a far greater variety of phrase-lengths in Symphonies 1 and 2—that is, before his vast symphonic conception took its first great step forward with Symphony No. 3.

Another general characteristic of Bruckner's style is his process of building a climax by means of sequential repetition. A Bruckner climax is a very individual thing, repeated phrases towering inexorably with almost cataclysmic effect. The real summit of each movement is enhanced by the way in which several previous pinnacles are averted and a new build-up started each time. Thus the ultimate culmination of these repeated periods of tension and release is remarkably effective. Bruckner's familiar unison themes always have a climactic character— for example the first movements of Symphony No. 9 (letter C) and Symphony No. 6 (after letter F).

His use of counterpoint in his symphonies is unobtrusive and unacademic. A great number of his themes invert, and many themes appear together with their own inversions. Often themes are developed in augmentation with their inversions in original note-values as a counterpoint. Diminution and fugato are also frequent procedures, contrapuntal lines being subtly dovetailed. Many of Bruckner's themes are 'double themes' and many of these are interlaced with new contrapuntal intricacies as they develop. A letter to Franz Bayer (organist and choirmaster at Steyr) of 22 April 1893 confirms that he felt symphonic counterpoint should be unobtrusive: 'I'm no pedal-point pusher—I don't give much for all that. Counterpoint isn't genius, only a means to an end. And it's given me plenty of trouble.' His melodic style reveals a fondness for dotted rhythms, scale progressions, and leaps, often of the fifth, sixth, and octave. One of his most striking melodic types is the chorale. He composed or incorporated chorales into vocal music as early as the St Florian period, such as *Dir, Herr, Dir will ich mich ergeben* (1844/5), *In jener letzten der Nächte* (*c.* 1848), *Entsagen* (*c.* 1851), and *Das edle Herz* (*c.* 1851). Chorale passages in the symphonies always have an important role to play. He was familiar with Lutheran chorales through his study of Bach, the works of other baroque composers, and Sechter. He may also have been influenced by Mendelssohn's use of the chorale in his *Lobgesang*, *St Paul*, and 'Reformation' Symphony. But he never used existing chorale melodies, only choralelike themes of his own invention. They appear either in the majesty of full brass or as a sublimely restful idea in the 'second group' of themes, and they occur in most of the symphonies after No. 3. Thematic unity has already been mentioned and will be illustrated in the discussion of the various symphonies. The culmination of themes in the finale is not the only example of this, however, and in the major-key symphonies (4, 5, 6, and 7) especially there are several examples of quotations of themes in other movements.

Pauses have become almost a notorious element in Bruckner's symphonies. At the first performance of Symphony No. 2 a member of the Vienna Philharmonic Orchestra dubbed it the 'Pausensinfonie'. Here again the pauses are an integral part of Bruckner's individual style. He replied to criticism of them by saying: 'Whenever I have something new and important to say, I must stop and take a breath first.' Naturally these pauses interrupt the flow of the music, but they are calculated to create a sense of anticipation and tension. They do not indicate a lack of ability to make a good transition, for excellent transitions can be found by only a cursory glance at the later Adagios; they emphasize the formal structure and can have either a dramatic or a wistful effect.

It is not possible to codify the form of Bruckner's symphonic movements. Any attempt to do so would have to qualify every statement made, as no symphony follows quite the same pattern as any other. Certain characteristics can be outlined, however. All the symphonies open quietly; Nos. 2, 4, 7, 8, and 9 with a tremolando and Nos. 3 and 6 with an ostinato. No. 5 has a slow introduction but the Allegro begins with a tremolando. Most of the first themes that emerge from this background of mystery are statements of fundamental harmonies, and the wonder lies in the fact that this 'formula' has a totally different character in each symphony. Nor do any of them sound like the prelude to *Das Rheingold*, although they share with it the evocation of creation itself, for example the opening of Symphony No. 4 (Ex. 3 overleaf).

Ex. 3

The finales of Nos. 6 and 7 begin with a tremolando and those of Nos. 2, 3, 4 and 8 with an ostinato.

Care and discretion must be taken in applying the terminology of sonata form to Bruckner's movements. We can for convenience refer to a 'first group' and 'second group' of themes, so long as we do not expect Bruckner to follow the classical pattern even in his expositions. A third thematic group becomes steadily more important and like the other two groups is composed of strongly contrasted material, although in some cases it is thematically related to them. As early as in the F minor 'study' symphony the outer movements contain prototype expositions of three thematic groups, the second song-like. The codas of both structures 'blaze-up' into impressive affirmations, the latter in the tonic major. In the finale of Symphony No. 2 the pattern of transition from exposition to development, which Bruckner follows in every succeeding outer movement, emerges. After a gigantic cadence marking the end of the first main section of the movement, the music remains still for a moment, ruminating gently on the foregoing thematic material, and so the development begins with slowly unfolding energy. A further word must be added about the second and third groups of themes. Bruckner's own term for his lyrical second group was *Gesangsperiode*, and themes in this group sometimes appear simultaneously, for example in the first movement of Symphony No. 3 (Ex. 4). The third group sometimes takes the form of a unison or 'double unison' theme, for example in the first movement of Symphony No. 7 (Ex. 5).

In using the terms 'recapitulation' and 'coda' we must be even more cautious. The recapitulation is never an orthodox repeat, but a new version of the exposition raised to a higher plane. The coda is vastly

Ex. 4

Ex. 5

extended and sums up everything in a mighty peroration. The second version of the first movement of Symphony No. 8 is the only outer movement to end quietly. From Symphony No. 3 onwards a process of telescoping the development and recapitulation begins, and finds its perfection in the first movement of Symphony No. 9, which defies any description of sonata form and can be discussed only in terms of Robert Simpson's apt phrase, 'statement, expanded counterstatement and coda'.

The Adagio movements do not have so many characteristics in common. In Symphonies 2 and 4 the slow movement is marked Andante, and in each symphony except Nos. 8 and 9 the slow movement follows the first movement. Most of the slow movements have two main thematic groups, and No. 6 is the only one in regular Brucknerian sonata form. The typical *Gesangsperiode* of the Adagios is a flowing lyrical idea which is embellished with ever richer accompaniment in its subsequent appearances.

The scherzos display the Austrian side of Bruckner most vividly. The earlier ones have the quality of peasant dances and the trio is frequently a Ländler. Here is an affinity with both Schubert, and Mahler. The Austrian elements in Bruckner's music have been both praised and denigrated very much according to the personal taste of the critic. In the main his treatment of them is neither obvious nor predictable, and their scale is never so extended as to upset the balance of the whole symphony. The second theme of the Scherzo of Symphony No. 5 is a good example. It never has a run of more than twenty bars or so and never upsets the symphonic context of the movement in a way that might well have happened if Mahler had developed it. Bruckner's early experiences as a dance-band fiddler may find their artistic fulfilment in these early scherzos, but the symphonic aspects of these movements become more pronounced after Symphony No. 4. In the Scherzo of Symphony No. 9 no trace is left of a peasant dance: a new and very different world is explored.

Bruckner's scherzos are never programme music, but they represent the nearest point he approached to it. That of Symphony No. 4 is marked 'Hunt Scherzo'. He did provide 'programmes' for Symphonies 4 and 8, but these are in quite a different category and amount to feeble afterthoughts, written to please his Wagnerian friends (who could not conceive of non-programmatic music) and brim with romantic effusions such as dawn, shady forests, horsemen galloping forth, and so on. He revealed his genuine view on this subject after Joseph Schalk provided a pictorial explanation of Symphony No. 7 for a Vienna performance. Bruckner angrily exclaimed: 'If he has to write poetry, why should he pick on my symphony?'

Bruckner's treatment of tonality is best seen in the context of each individual work, but one or two general points may be made here. He had a fondness for Neapolitan relationships, finely illustrated in the String Quintet and Symphony No. 6, but evident in almost every mature work. Rapid changes of tonality are a feature of his sequences, which often rise in steps of a semitone. Harmony and tonality are his most striking points in common with Schubert. In both composers the key relationships between the first- and second-subject groups are unconventional. Mediant instead of dominant relationships are favoured and they both exploit sudden changes from major chords or tonalities to minor ones. For both men harmony was as much an agent of expression as melody and rhythm, and Bruckner's expansiveness of form is due to the enlarged modulatory possibilities of his style. 'Heavenly length', recurrence of themes, statements of the second group in two melodic strands, and the Austrian quality of some melodies are further points in common with Schubert. They have very few resemblances in the realms of orchestration, counterpoint, or rhythm. It is doubtful whether all the elements of kinship between Schubert and Bruckner were the direct result of Bruckner's knowledge of Schubert's work. In Bruckner's formative years Schubert's Masses and symphonies were unpopular, and his knowledge of Schubert was at that time largely confined to songs and piano music. But the strong affinity between these two composers lies at a deep level and cannot be explained in terms of direct influence.

Finally, the difference between the symphonic conception of Bruckner and Mahler respectively ought to be considered. The two men were very different in personality, and this is reflected in their scores. Mahler's life and character are dominated by *Weltschmerz*, pessimism, unrest, irony, and a longing for escape. The programmatic element in Mahler's symphonies is important. Mahler was a complex, obsessive, and searching religious mystic. Bruckner, his senior by thirty-six years, shares very little of all this. His faith was a mysticism of quite a different order. He had found his God, and with Him repose and serenity. However, Mahler undoubtedly inherited a number of superficial points of style from Bruckner. These include the rustic elements found in the earlier scherzos of both composers, long song-like melodies as in Bruckner's 'second-group' themes, a fondness for rugged, stubborn march rhythms and the symphonic time-scale. But in the realms of expression, orchestration, and general symphonic shape there is a vast gulf between Bruckner and Mahler.

An Austrian symphonist nearer to Bruckner in style is Franz Schmidt (1874–1939). Schmidt's four symphonies should be far better known and in some respects they are worthy successors to Bruckner's nine. He studied at the Vienna Conservatory, 1889–96, and was a pupil of Bruckner, but for only a very short time. Another Bruckner student was Emile Jacques-Dalcroze (born of French parents in Vienna in 1865; died in Geneva, 1950), composer of operas, ballets, piano music, and many other works, and the creator of 'Eurythmics'. A significant heir to the Bruckner tradition was Richard Wetz (1875–1935), composer of three symphonies, teacher, and a biographer of Bruckner. Friedrich Klose, well-known as author of reminiscences of his teacher Bruckner, wrote symphonic poems, choral and chamber works which are worthy of performance. The long-delayed première of the uneven but striking Symphony by another Bruckner pupil, Hans Rott, in 1989, revealed an extraordinary link between Bruckner and Mahler. Lastly, the Masses and other church music by another member of Bruckner's circle, his friend Josef Wöss, are also worthy of notice.

11

Smaller works and chamber music

Bruckner composed over thirty male-voice choruses in addition to a number of secular works for mixed chorus. They are of little concern to the non-German listener and do not represent important stages in Bruckner's creative unfolding. They are the side-products of his art; pieces that could be readily and frequently performed. Most of them were written for specific choral groups. The most important male-voice choruses include *Am Grabe* (1861), *Germanenzug* (1863), *Das deutsche Lied* (1892), and a symphonic chorus with large orchestra, *Helgoland* (1893). *Am Grabe* was the first work written for the *Liedertafel* '*Frohsinn*' after his appointment as conductor. It has the distinction of being his first work to be performed in Linz and to receive a press notice in the *Linzer Zeitung*: 'the entire composition is imbued with tender emotion and unshakeable faith in God'. August Silberstein's *Germanenzug* ('Germanen durchschreiten des Urwaldes Nacht') is scored for fifteen brass instruments; the poem celebrates the Teutonic deities Odin, Freya, and the Walkyre-maidens. Perhaps *Abendzauber* (1878) is the best example from the whole genre of male voice works to mention, as it sums up the purely romantic spirit that they all share. It is set for baritone solo and three yodellers, and the accompaniment consists of four horns. Austrian folk elements abound in choruses such as this, and thus a tenuous link is formed with some of the symphonic scherzos.

Helgoland was the only secular vocal composition that Bruckner included in his bequest to the *Hofbibliothek*. It was his last completed work, written for the fiftieth anniversary of the Vienna Male Choir, to whom he dedicated it. Silberstein is again the poet of this grandiose ballad in which he depicts the proud, small, rocky island fortress in the North Sea which had only recently been ceded to Germany by Britain (in an imperialistic exchange for Zanzibar!). Nationalist pride is metamorphosed into a vision of the ancient 'Saxon isle' threatened by Roman invasion. The inhabitants implore the intervention of God, who unleashes an almighty tempest over the waters, shattering the foe and restoring peace and security to Heligoland. To this vivid miniature drama (thirteen minutes of music) Bruckner applies a thrilling succession of orchestral gestures familiar from the later symphonies: surging and cascading string writing, robust paeans of brass, arresting choral unisons. Yet it is not all pictorial storm and stress: a judicious balance of reflective, quieter passages affords lyrical contrast. The orchestral transition to the final words, 'O Herrgott, dich preiset frei Helgoland', reminiscent of the opening theme of the Seventh Symphony, is particularly impressive.

The only direct link between Bruckner's many affairs of the heart and his creative work is found in the small group of songs and piano pieces that they inspired. The influence of Schubert and also of Schumann (whose songs he came to know at the time of his studies with Sechter and his friendship with the Mayfelds who were ardent Schumann enthusiasts) can be seen in the three songs of the late 1860s—'Im April', 'Mein Herz und deine Stimme', and 'Herbstkummer'. The last, with its varied accompaniment, is the best of the group. The piano pieces are quite pleasant, very Austrian and undistinguished. They are mostly dance-like pieces except for the Fantasie in G (1868) with its slow introduction reminiscent of Liszt and oddly contrasting Allegro in rococo style, and *Erinnerung* of about the same date, which is an ambitious piece with interesting harmonies.

Bruckner is one of a relatively small number of great composers whose chief performing talent lay in the organ-loft. Unlike Franck or Reger, however, he has not left a single composition of any value for his instrument. The C minor Prelude and Fugue of 1847 has nothing more than Mendelssohn in it, and his last organ work proper, the D minor Fugue of 1861, is academic and uninspired. Sadly, we have no record of his famous improvisations (except for several prosy descriptions of them), but these were to bear fruit in other, more significant ways. The organ was an essential stepping-stone for Bruckner's creative imagination.

The Overture in G minor of 1863 is the only orchestral work of interest in his output aside from the symphonies. It is an enormous improvement on the three short pieces for orchestra that slightly preceded it. Cast in straightforward sonata form, it has a slow introduction notable for its strong descending octaves, reminiscent of Mozart's 'Jupiter' Symphony, striking harmonic suspensions and chromaticism. There is a fine example of a typical Bruckner crescendo or 'blaze-up' using the first-subject material (at figure 14 in the Universal Edition score). The second subject should be noted. Beginning on the dominant ninth chord of B flat major, this is only a glimmer of the *Gesangsperioden* to come, but a glimmer that has the glance of hidden gold.

The String Quartet in C minor of the previous year is a delightful work, worthy of occasional performance, which was discovered only after World War II. The key itself is significant—he was later to choose it for three of his symphonies. The trio of the third movement has a Schubertian, freshly bucolic charm. The Quartet is, however, merely an advanced exercise in composition, showing that Bruckner had a firm grasp of traditional forms, proficiency in string writing, and a thoughtful way of developing thematic material. Bruckner wrote an alternative Rondo finale for the Quartet, on a somewhat larger scale, which has also been published.

His single important chamber work is the String Quintet in F major which he composed between Symphonies 5 and 6. It is by no means a 'symphony for five strings' and it never stretches the quintet medium beyond its capabilities, save perhaps for the last seventeen bars of the finale, where he is thinking too much in orchestral terms. The Quintet is unlike any other late nineteenth-century chamber music; though Brahms's Op. 88 (written two and a half years later in 1882) shares the key of Bruckner's, the layout of 2 violins, 2 violas, and cello, and the idea of contrapuntal devices in the finale, the two works have little in common. Yet Bruckner's Quintet is a worthy companion not only of the chamber music of Brahms but of late Beethoven and Schubert also. The Adagio is one of his most profound movements and illustrates perfectly how well at home he was in a chamber-music medium. Throughout the Quintet fascinating Neapolitan relationships abound. This is evident from the very outset; so many Bruckner movements hint, in their very first bars, at the tonality to be explored. Note the A flat and D flat in the first bar (Ex. 6). The flat submediant key, D flat, makes itself strongly felt throughout the whole work. F sharp or G flat major (the Neapolitan flat supertonic of F) is likewise important, and this is the key of the second thematic group of the first movement (letter E). The Scherzo, a tour-de-force of droll wit and harmonic sleight of hand, is in D minor (a key entirely avoided in the opening movement) and its first section ends on the dominant, A. B flat major immediately takes over, and both G flat and D flat are encountered before the final cadence in D major. The capriciously graceful Trio then starts on the Neapolitan flat supertonic of D, E flat major, and its central section is in G flat, which is again the key of the Adagio. Although the Scherzo is beyond any doubt the right movement for this Quintet, one feels almost grateful to Hellmesberger for objecting to it, as this brought forth the exquis-

Ex. 6

itely poised Intermezzo. Once again this movement (in D minor) contains some fine ebb and flow with G flat major. (The Trio was not altered.) The order of movements was originally Adagio then Scherzo, but Bruckner altered their places and thus created a better approach to the finale which opens on a dominant ninth in G flat (the key signature is A flat) and only zig-zags its way back to F by means of an audacious odyssey via every foreign port until it reaches home waters. Throughout the Quintet the ear is held spell-bound through the effect of these devious but ingeniously determined tonal relations, which permeate both the smallest detail and the broad spectrum. Lest the reader worry that this work is no more than a display of harmonic cunning, then it should be stressed that no other piece in Bruckner's output rivals it for melodic richness and variety. Ex. 7 illustrates the two great, unhurried main themes of the third movement. (Note the identical rhythm of their first bars.) Both melodies bear the seeds of elaborately inventive development. The finale (*Lebhaft bewegt*) contains three main thematic groups, the first never appearing again until close to the work's end (and to great dramatic effect), the second a luxuriant five-stranded *Gesangsperiode*, and the third beginning as an earnest fugue but unbending slowly to

Ex. 7

release its lyric beauty. The Quintet is a work of breathtaking originality; the spontaneity of its composition, the easy confidence with which
he handles the chamber medium, and the audacious use of tonal
antipodes and harmonic contradictions belie the astonishing fact that its
creator had at that time never heard any of the late quartets of
Beethoven (whom, by the way, it does not resemble).

12

The early symphonies in minor keys

The *Studiensimphonie* (Study Symphony) in F minor (1863) was never performed in Bruckner's lifetime and the composer regarded it as nothing more than an exercise. He wrote 'Schularbeit' on a copy of the score now in the Vienna *Staatsbibliothek*. Following such rigorous self-criticism this work has previously been perhaps too quickly dismissed as the impersonal, stiff, conventional product of the schoolroom. Set beside the Overture in G minor it is certainly thematically uninspired and less characterful. Yet, given an occasional sympathetic airing, it has the power to convince, with some moments of warm melodiousness and consistently fine if unoriginal scoring. There are especially effective touches of solo woodwind and horn, as well as of full brass and string writing that reveal how well Bruckner had responded to Kitzler's emphasis on the importance of orchestral colour. The large scale of the work is characteristic of Bruckner's hand, as are several features of style, if not yet of form: the outer sections of the admirably vital Scherzo are already unmistakably Brucknerian; the massive chorale-like chords which punctuate phrases of the felicitous opening theme throughout the movement; and the coda to the movement (approached by an increasingly effective web of contrapuntal strands) which develops a reiterated falling figure strikingly anticipatory (in rhythm and direction, if not in mood or dynamic) of that contained in the equivalent passage of Symphony No. 8, 1890 version (Ex. 8). Both coda-figures are derived from their movements' first subjects. The coda to the Andante is also noteworthy for its unexpected heightening of the potential beauties of the main theme; and the coda of the (otherwise rather academic) finale is one of the finest moments, foreshadowing the opening of Symphony No. 0 in its figuration, and containing a chorale-like motif later used in the Mass in D minor.

Bruckner called his official Symphony No. 1 in C minor 'das kecke Beserl'—an untranslatable phrase, the 'cheeky' or 'saucy little besom', or 'minx' or 'shrew', being the nearest equivalents—and this portrays in a nutshell the jaunty, impertinent character of the opening idea and the bold impetuosity of the Scherzo. Both the outer movements are faster in tempo than is usual in Bruckner's symphonies, and the boisterous

Ex. 8

(a) Symphony in F minor: Coda to 1st movement

(b) Symphony No. 8 (1890): Coda to 1st movement

spirit and vigour of the finale particularly justify the composer's later astonishment at the dash and daring of the piece. But again, there are many pointers to the later works to be observed here, and they mark the finest moments in the score. Augmentation, even double-augmentation of phrases, is frequent, as are characteristic shifts of timbre from one orchestral plane to another (for example bars 50–60 of the opening Allegro). The string writing is immensely assured. The second group of the first movement begins most effectively in uncomplicated two-part writing, is embellished in a restatement and leads to a characteristic tutti. Out of this tutti (which announces the rhythmic pattern of the main theme of the finale in the brass) emerges a strong idea on trombones and in a broader tempo in E flat major (letter C) which, with its accompanying string demisemiquaver figure (shades of *Tannhäuser*), provides powerful building material for the development, after which it does not reappear. The transition to the recapitulation is a fine stroke, the home dominant key emerging for the first time in the movement, and the movement ends with idiosyncratic finality. The Adagio is in A flat major, but its opening gives no hint of this. Here is an inkling of the technique used in the Adagio of Symphony No. 9. The ambiguous harmony first gropes darkly towards F minor, then lifts twice in mysterious directions before any clear sign of the tonic key emerges. Only in the last eighteen bars does A flat major again claim its rightful place, and this beautiful and dignified movement closes in tranquillity. There also exists a substantial fragment of an abandoned Adagio which shares thematic ideas with the final version, but unlike it was to be cast in classical sonata form with development, whereas the finished form is ternary ABA. A is a sonata exposition with two main ideas which return in heightened recapitulatory development after B, an elaborately constructed middle section. The G minor of the Scherzo and the G major of the Trio are fresh tonal realms, and so the impetuous outburst of the Scherzo is doubly unsuspected after the calm of the Adagio's final A flat major. The Scherzo's irregularity of phrase lengths, especially at the opening, is noteworthy. This movement, too, replaced a rejected one, also in G minor, and much shorter, although with equally skittish metrical irregularity (two-beat phrases against the three-in-the-bar). The Trio was retained with some small alterations in instrumentation, and is at a welcome strolling pace after the ceaseless momentum of the Scherzo. The coda to the Scherzo repeat restores G major. Later, Bruckner preferred a mysterious, shimmering or lustrous preliminary background to his finales and criticized his naïvety in this example for appearing at once with his forceful main idea as if some fool had barged into a room and cried loudly 'Da bin i'!' ('Here I am!'). Yet its boldness is at one with the spirit of the whole symphony. In the finale there is a good example of Bruckner's technique of slowly building up energy at the beginning of the development after some reflections on the cadence figure of the exposition. The work ends with a chorale-like blaze of glory on the horns. The First Symphony is unique amongst its companions discussed in this chapter in having no thematic allusions to the sacred choral works.

It is necessary to comment briefly on the 1891 version of the work ('Vienna' version), although the 'Linz' version is most usually played today. Bruckner did revise it of his own volition despite the fact that Bülow and Rubinstein had admired the Linz version and Levi even urged him not to alter his original ideas. He bequeathed both versions of the score to the *Hofbibliothek*. The main differences in the later score are found in harmony, counterpoint, scoring, texture, altered bar-periods, extra tempo-markings and the rewriting of certain sections, including the end of the finale. The result of all this was effectively to destroy the charm and natural exuberance of his youthful style.

When Otto Dessoff rehearsed Bruckner's early Symphony in D minor with the Vienna Philharmonic Orchestra, he turned to the composer and asked him to tell him where the first subject of the opening movement was. This reception of the work may lie behind Bruckner's decision not to include it amongst his numbered symphonies. Yet *'die Nullte'* is a most individual work, a great creative step forward, and the opening which puzzled Dessoff is the first truly Brucknerian symphonic ostinato.[1] He used it again to open Symphony No. 3, where it forms a background to the principal theme. The reason why Symphony No. 0 reveals Bruckner's personality so clearly is that it was written in 1869—that is, three years after Symphony No. 1, and after his coming to know Beethoven's Ninth. The possibility of its existence in an earlier draft (most likely of 1863–4) cannot be discounted and is accepted by authorities as distinguished as Haas, Nowak, Cooke, and Simpson. The first movement is the most remarkable and shows many traces of his experience of Beethoven's last symphony, for example in the descending fifths and fourths at the opening, over a drone of an open fifth. Another link with the Choral Symphony is the chromatic ostinato at the beginning of the coda—a device which Bruckner was to use again in the first movement of Symphony No. 3 and also in the finale of Symphony No. 6, where it re-appears literally as in No. 0. Other features to be noticed in this first movement are the excellent second group, the reverent procession of chorales, and the beginning of the development which grows naturally out of the cadence of the exposition—a feature that finds further expression in the next symphony, No. 2 in C minor. No. 0 also shares with No. 2 the procedure of quotation from the sacred choral works. The staccato quavers from the 'Gratias' of the Mass in F minor propel the development of the first movement. The Andante includes two statements of the 'Qui tollis peccata mundi' from the Mass in E minor. The finale quotes the 'Osanna' of the early Requiem in D minor (at letter A) and the seven-part setting of the 'Ave Maria' appears at the transition from development to recapitulation. The symphony itself was drawn on for thematic material in later symphonies.

That Symphony No. 2 is in C minor has actually been cited as a proof of Bruckner's naïvety as a composer. 'After all, who would write his first two symphonies in the same key?' sneers the enemy. Here, as so often, the enemy's zeal outstrips his intelligence. Just over five busy years separate the two works—years that saw the creation of the Masses in E minor and F minor and the writing of the definitive version of Symphony No. 0 in D minor. Furthermore the two symphonies share little more than their key-signature. The impetuous qualities of No. 1 find few echoes in No. 2. The slow deliberate mastery of later years is not yet achieved, but the essence of Bruckner's style is far more apparent. Over a tremolando tonic chord the opening theme feels its way into C minor, and towards the end of its twenty-three bar span the trumpet throws out the 'Bruckner rhythm' in dotted values, on the note C. The whole theme

---

[1] This characteristic ostinato is prefigured in his setting of Psalm 146 (1860).

is then expanded in a varied counterstatement. The 'Bruckner rhythm' never takes on a melodic shape during the symphony. Its use is structural in the first movement and the finale. The second groups of themes in both outer movements enjoy a few adventures of tonality. In the first movement the second group appears at first, quite properly, in E flat major. In the development it explores both G and A flat major before arriving in D flat major, and in the recapitulation finds a happy resting place in C major. In the finale the second group enters in A major, although the way prepared for it pointed to A flat. However, it effortlessly finds its way into E flat in its own measured time. It, too, appears in C major in the recapitulation, but here the delight is an even fresher surprise: it follows a dominant-seventh chord of D flat major. Both second groups are characteristically lyrical, flowing and gentle. The third thematic group of the first movement restores the drive and impetus of the music with a stark double unison (Ex. 9). The ostinato figure from

Ex. 9

Ex. 9 takes on an augmented form in the development and appears over another ostinato. The coda, as in Beethoven's Ninth, begins over an ostinato bass.[2] Typically, the coda is two-fold. The first and greater part of it is development of the opening theme, and the second (at the final return of Tempo I) is a mighty tutti in C minor.

The Adagio clearly illustrates Bruckner's favourite slow movement process of enhancing the restatements of his two main themes by elaborating and enriching the accompanying figuration, over a spacious 'ABABA + Coda' plan. There are two quotations from the Benedictus of the Mass in F minor. The finale has two similar quotations from the

[2] The optional cut suggested here in the Haas edition should not be observed as it would take us too quickly and uncertainly to C minor and upset the proportions of the whole movement. The same logic applies to the optional cuts towards the end of the finale (these cuts are observed in Nowak's score).

Kyrie of the same Mass and is linked to the first movement in a number of ways. The ostinato figure with which it opens is derived from the opening theme of the symphony; this theme itself appears during the development, first in a transformed version, then in its original form and finally grows into a new melody. It also finds its place in the coda. The 'Bruckner rhythm' also links the outer movements, appearing at a number of climactic points including the final C major peroration. The emphatic rhythm of the coda to the taut Scherzo is electrifying, and another hint of things to come. The Trio yodels all cares away with a winning tune. The explanation of the pauses and of the less daring character of this symphony lies in Dessoff's criticism of Symphonies 0 and 1. The pauses were Bruckner's attempt at emphasizing his formal structure: they in no way detract from the greatness of the work. He has now climbed the foothills: the Himalayas lie ahead.

That new territory is to be explored is obvious from the beginning of Symphony No. 3 in D minor, where the broad tempo and extended thematic dimensions at once suggest a different time-scale. After four bars in which a multiple ostinato grows, the trumpet announces the principal subject (Ex. 10a). The horn then expands this figure and a crescendo leads to an important unison idea (Ex. 10b), its mighty falling fortissimo given out by full orchestra, followed by its quiet inversion on strings alone, which is immediately restated in rich harmonies. One of the most captivating features of this first movement is the way in which this motif recurs, always in a new harmonization. Its first unison entry follows thirty bars of tonic pedal. This is a feature of Bruckner's openings that will be observed again. The restatement of the opening material is in the

Ex. 10

(a)

(b)

dominant key, again over a pedal bass, and the second group (at bar 135 in the 1873 score, see Ex. 4) is also characterized by a held pedal bass. This second group contains the 'Bruckner rhythm' (which was implied in the first theme) and, using this, a crescendo leads to the third theme, a firm unison which also shares the 'Bruckner rhythm'. Shortly before the development there is a brief quotation of the 'Miserere' from the Mass in D minor, and in the transition to the development a theme from Symphony No. 2 appears. Towards the end of the exposition, and during the remainder of the movement, Ex. 10a is stated in inversion and augmentation, and in canon using both of these devices. In every respect the 1873 score is superior to the later revisions. This is true also of the Adagio, which in 1877 is spoiled by relentless one-, two-, and four-bar phrases, yet in both versions it has a noble climax—the worthy predecessor of those in almost all succeeding symphonies. The opening theme of the E flat major slow movement has a classical simplicity and warmth. Later some use is made of a cadence common in Viennese Classical sacred music (Ex. 11). Bruckner had previously used this *Marienkadenz* in the four-part Ave Maria of 1856, the seven-part Ave Maria of 1861, the Agnus Dei of the Mass in F minor and the piano piece *Erinnerung* of 1868.

Ex. 11

As to the much-vaunted Wagner quotations, these are subtly and delicately integrated. A hushed reminiscence of the 'sleep motif' from *Die Walküre* Act 3 is woven into the development of the opening movement and returns at the close of the Adagio which, much earlier, contained veiled references to the chromatic opening phrase of *Tristan*. (I can also detect a whiff of smoke from Loge's fire in the finale.) It should be emphasized that, even in 1873, these quotations are of passing interest. The truly arresting features are all Bruckner's own in the first two movements and are given proper room to expand organically, as opposed to the 1877 revision's cutting back, pruning, and even uprooting of the natural growth. The D minor Scherzo, too, is very much Bruckner's own: the rhythms of its fine-knit first subject are more artfully designed in 1873 than later, its second subject is a Ländler (which Mahler seems to remember affectionately in his First Symphony). The A major Trio is also a Ländler of delightful contrast, lean, spry, and nimble-footed.

The colossal 'allegro' finale (764 bars in 1873) is architecturally Bruckner's most audacious structure to date and he holds its vast spaces together with awe-inspiring integration. The idiosyncratic first theme emerges from a whirlwind ostinato of rising quavers. The second theme appears surprisingly in F sharp major. It is a double theme; the strings play a polka while the horns intone a chorale. August Göllerich recalls an occasion when Bruckner commented on this unusual combination. He and Bruckner were walking past a house in the Schottenring one evening and they overheard dance music. Not far away the body of the cathedral architect Schmidt lay in the Sühnhaus. Bruckner remarked: 'Listen! In that house there is dancing, and over there the master lies in his coffin—that's life. It's what I wanted to show in my Third Symphony. The polka represents the fun and joy of the world and the chorale represents the sadness and pain.'[3]

The principal weakness of the 1877 version of this symphony is a problem of form. With this work the process of telescoping the development and recapitulation begins, and Bruckner's misjudgement was to so alter his proportions that neither the opening movement nor the finale has a successful recapitulatory climax. In both movements in 1877 the recapitulation is forestalled by a massive statement of Ex. 10a in the development section in the tonic key. In both cases the momentum of the rest of the movement is destroyed and all ensuing climaxes have a weak effect.

The 1890 version of the symphony fails to solve these structural weaknesses. Several of the tutti passages are altered in the later score with some success, but few of the 'improvements' are impressive. Rescoring of brass parts, altering of bar-periods, large cuts, and a bombastic coda to the finale amount to the loss of a number of fine effects and the gain of nothing but a desire to hear Ex. 10a draw the work to an end. It is much to be regretted that conductors still choose this last revision in preference to the original, which has been available since 1977.

---

[3] Göllerich–Auer IV/2, p. 663.

13

Sacred vocal works

Bruckner completed seven Masses including his Requiem. The first two of these date from the early 1840s and are typical examples of the short provincial Austrian *Landmesse* of the day. The Windhaag Mass in C major of 1842 is for alto, two horns, and organ, the organ accompaniment being written as a figured bass. Parts of the text are cut, particularly the Credo. Like every Mass which followed, this early example shows the use of themes influenced by plainsong, and chromaticism for pictorial effect. The opening of the Credo is a plainsong quotation, while only a few bars later, at the words 'qui propter nostram salutem descendit de coelis', Bruckner gives a chromatic response. The Benedictus contains a clear trace of Mozart's influence. The Kronstorf Mass in F major for Maundy Thursday of 1844 is very similar to the C major Mass and shows plainsong influence, but suffers even more from crippling local conditions. There is no Kyrie or Gloria but a Gradual, 'Christus factus est', and an Offertory, 'Dextera Domini fecit virtutem', are interpolated. A number of interesting points of imitation occur in the generally homophonic texture, and in the Osanna there are effective leaps of the seventh and a tendency towards dissonance and unorthodox modulation. The work is headed with the letters, so significant in later works, A.m.D.g.—Ad majorem Dei gloriam.

The fragment of an unfinished Mass in E flat major, for chorus, orchestra, and organ, of about 1846, shows a more ambitious approach to choral and instrumental writing. There are antiphonal responses for soloists and chorus and the vocal parts are laid out in a less amateurish way. Of the motets of the 1840s, three settings of 'Asperges me' (1843–5) and the 'Tantum ergo' in A major deserve a mention. The F major 'Asperges me' (WAB 4) formerly thought to be of the late Linz years, has now been convincingly re-dated to almost a quarter of a century earlier, that is to Bruckner's Kronstorf period.[1] It is an excellent early example of how Bruckner can base a work almost entirely on a plainsong outline and yet transform his material with chromatic harmony and melodic inflections. The first of the two 'Asperges me' (WAB 3) is an

[1] *Bruckner Gesamtausgabe*, Vol. 21: *Kleine Kirchenmusikwerke. Revisionsbericht*, ed. Nowak (Vienna, 1984), p. 11.

Aeolian setting that begins polyphonically; its companion, inspired by plainsong, is a hymn in two sections which flank a verse of unharmonized plainsong. The 'Tantum ergo' moves from A major to D sharp (enharmonic E flat major—the polar opposite of A) at the climax of a central imitative section and returns to A by way of B major.

With the Requiem in D minor, for soloists, chorus, orchestra, and organ of 1848–9, we leave juvenilia behind. The key remained a significant one for Bruckner until his last symphony, and this Requiem may be regarded as his first truly notable composition, well worthy of performance. He always retained a regard for it and made some revisions to the score as late as 1894, commenting: 'It isn't bad.' Haydn and Mozart are his principal models, particularly Mozart's Requiem in the same key, to which there are a number of thematic allusions. The opening theme of the Requiem is almost identical to the opening of Mozart's. At 'donum fac remissionis' in Bruckner, Mozart's 'Ne absorbeat eas tartarus' is quoted, and at 'defunctorum de poenis' the theme of Mozart's 'de ore leonis' appears. But Bruckner's own voice is assuredly to the fore. Scored for three trombones, strings, and organ continuo (with a horn replacing one trombone in the Benedictus), the orchestral effect is austere, yet the festal Mass style of his later mature period is anticipated. Dark string syncopations accompany the opening choral passage. The 'Hostias' is tellingly laid out for divided tenors and basses, with well judged contributions from his favourite three trombones. 'Quam olim Abrahae' is a great double fugue using the unexpected key of F minor. The Benedictus and Agnus Dei particularly reveal profound depths of expression.

The Magnificat in B flat major of 1852 is also scored austerely for two trumpets, three trombones, strings, and organ. It contains a fine fugal Amen. The settings of Psalms 22 and 114 also culminate in impressive fugues, the latter in a fine double fugue. Both show the influence of Mendelssohn and, in Psalm 22, of Schubert. Psalm 144 reveals features that with hindsight can be styled Brucknerian: wide vocal leaps enhancing vivid word-setting (for example at the words 'Es umgaben mich die Schmerzen des Todes'—'the pains of death encompassed me') and pictorial emphasis by use of the three trombones. Contrapuntal work distinguishes the 'Libera' in F minor of 1854, which again makes dramatic use of trombones, low strings, and organ. The next real landmark in the evolution of Bruckner's choral and orchestral style is the Missa Solemnis in the bold dark key of B flat minor. Here the influence of the Masses of Michael and Joseph Haydn and of Mozart is still strong, and the composer's individuality is not so clearly evident as in the Requiem, although the Mass certainly deserves performance. Friedrich Mayr, its dedicatee, had been director of the monastery of St Florian (1825–48) during Prelate Arneth's reign. He had promised Bruckner, when the latter was still assistant teacher at Kronstorf, to return him to St Florian whenever he passed the necessary teacher's examination. This promise prompted Bruckner's composition of the cantata significantly entitled *Vergissmein-nicht* (Forget-me-not). Mayr was true to his word and his own return to St Florian, as head of the monastic foundation in 1854, must have given Bruckner added impetus in the creation of this Missa Solemnis, his largest work yet for chorus and orchestra. Bruckner uses a richer orchestral palette in this Mass (adding two oboes, two bassoons, and timpani to the orchestra used for the Magnificat) which was partly an elaboration of sketches made in his Kronstorf years. The opening phrase of the Kyrie, although merely a rising and falling minor third, will raise a prescient eyebrow in the listener who knows the start of the Ninth Symphony. Oboe and cello lines add character to the 'Qui tollis'. The Credo contains effectively dramatic use of ascending chromaticism at 'Et resurrexit' and ends with a fine triple fugue at 'Et vitam venturi', which is thematically linked with the opening. This fugue has the characteristics of those in the three great Masses, such as inversion of the subject and an effective entry of the soloists just before the end. Owing to the discovery of the original parts (which Bruckner completed on his thirtieth birthday) Nowak's edition is more consistent and detailed than earlier ones. In his preface Nowak rightly remarks that

> though he was thirty years old . . . he had been given no regular tuition in this type of composition. The Bruckner of 1854 can in fact be regarded as self-taught, as his studies with Dürrnberger and Zenetti were limited to thorough-bass, harmony, organ, and the elements of counterpoint. Any progress he made beyond these rudimentary studies was due entirely to his own diligence and thirst for knowledge. He is known to have spent hours on end at the organ or piano, and from one or two exercise-folios that have survived we can appreciate how assiduously he studied the works of the great masters, especially as regards counterpoint: while still in Linz he copied out Bach's *Kunst der Fuge*. The Missa Solemnis can therefore be regarded as the *summa musices* of the first thirty years of Bruckner's life . . . Its germ of creative ability was so pronounced that it was on the grounds of this Mass alone that Simon Sechter in 1855 had no hesitation in accepting Bruckner as a pupil.

Shortly after leaving St Florian Bruckner wrote an 'Ave Maria' in F major for soloists, mixed chorus, and organ, dedicated to the choirmaster there, Ignaz Traumihler. This piece, which contains some fine chromatic moments, was the last sacred work before he completed his period of study with Sechter, and all those works that follow command more attention. Psalm 146 of 1860 uses a large orchestra and is in the style of a cantata. Two motets of 1861 illustrate that Bruckner had thoroughly mastered complex contrapuntal writing with Sechter. 'Afferentur regi' contains a characteristic leap in the bass part to a low A pedal note at 'et exsultatione'. The seven-part 'Ave Maria' is the first masterpiece among the motets—a fine piece of contrapuntal weaving clearly showing Bruckner's Palestrinian ancestry and yet allowing free reign to his own chromatic richness. The three-part female chorus enters alone, followed by the four-part male chorus, and then all parts join in a solemn climax (see Ex. 12). Similar strength of harmonic device can be seen in Psalm 112 for double chorus and orchestra of 1863. This opens (like Bruckner's next psalm setting of nearly thirty years later) with exuberant cries of 'Allelujah!' Set in B flat major and cast in ABA form, its first section includes an anticipation of the slow movement of Symphony No. 2, and the start of 'B' looks forward to the Benedictus of his next great Mass. If the spirits of Schubert and Mendelssohn still hover nearby, Psalm 112 is none the less thoroughly integrated, with a new confidence and easy fluency of mood painting. The reprise embraces a radiant fugue.

Bruckner's first work of symphonic grandeur is the Mass in D minor of 1864, a traditional Austrian festal Mass which he revised in 1876 and 1881. The opening of the Kyrie is a string passage over a tonic pedal, rich in dissonance and remote harmonies, but never straying away from D minor. The first Kyrie introduces an ascending scale that is a unifying element throughout the Mass, appearing at the opening of the Gloria and Sanctus, in descending form in the Benedictus, and in both forms in the Agnus Dei. The more imitative and varied second Kyrie contains an octave figure that is another link between the various movements and recurs in the Gloria, Credo, and Sanctus. (Scale motifs and octave leaps are also a unifying feature of Psalm 150.) The first lines of both Gloria and Credo are reserved for plainsong intonation as in the Mass in E minor. The Gloria in D major opens dramatically with chromatic crotchet movement in the bass, soon replaced by pervading diatonic quaver scales. The central 'Agnus Dei' section of the Gloria opens in an unexpected A flat major, and the 'miserere' motif appears in both Symphonies 3 and 9. As in the E minor and F minor Masses, this movement ends with a fugue, which includes stretto and stretto by inversion. The symphonic elements are most clearly seen in the Credo, also in D major. The central 'et incarnatus est' section (Adagio) begins with a dramatic entry of the soloists in F sharp major. The vocal parts climb chromatically in a unison climax towards a D major six-three chord at 'ex Maria Virgine', and 'et homo factus est' cadences wonderfully in C major. After a vigorous 'Crucifixus', the entry of pianissimo organ and quiet solo voices at 'et sepultus est' is a most effective change of colour, and so is the dark descending chromatic figure at 'mortuorum'—an effect almost identical to the setting of that word in the Mass in F minor. 'Et resurrexit' is approached by way of a symphonic orchestral introduction of twenty-eight bars on the home dominant, almost reminiscent of Symphony No. 1 with its tramping bass ostinato and broken phrases of dotted quavers growing in momentum. As in the Missa Solemnis and in the next two Masses, the resurrection episode drew from Bruckner some of his most sublime music. The G major Benedictus has a sixteen-

Ex. 12

bar introduction of graceful poise, and flowing accompaniment and interludes enhance this pastoral movement. It hovers in C sharp major at the close, almost suggesting a vision of the Holy Spirit, when the chorus enter boldly with the reprise of the Hosanna in D. The thematic summing-up of all that has gone before, in the Agnus Dei, has been discussed in Chapter 10. In the outer movements of all three Masses of the 1860s sheer display is dispensed with entirely; these movements have an inner solemnity and are linked thematically.[2]

The Mass in E minor of 1866 is the most individual and perhaps the finest of the three great Masses of this period, and stands apart from almost all other nineteenth-century liturgical music by virtue of the forces it employs and its peculiarly expressive harmonic and contrapuntal language. It was first performed in the open air on the occasion of the consecration of the Votive Chapel for the new cathedral in Linz. The authentic performing version is that of 1882, which followed two revisions, of 1869 and 1876. The Mass employs an eight-part mixed chorus and a wind band of two oboes, two clarinets, four horns, two trumpets and three trombones—a notable combination making no use of timpani, organ or soloists and not paralleled in any other Bruckner work. This orchestra is used sparingly in a background role, yet it contributes wonderfully to the striking contrasts of texture and constant variety of sound. In the Gloria the opening bassoon arpeggio figure sets in motion the forward-moving repeated crotchet pattern that propels the whole structure, while step-wise and repeated quaver patterns perform a similar function in the Credo. In the Benedictus and Agnus Dei the orchestra weaves its own threads into the intricate texture of the tapestry and forms an unbroken link between the vocal phrases, while in the Kyrie and Christe and at the climax of the Sanctus it powerfully reinforces and highlights moments of the vocal declamation of the text.

No work of Bruckner's illustrates so succinctly his unique position amongst composers since the Baroque era. Here is music of profound wisdom conveyed with utmost simplicity of expression that embraces romantic, fully Brucknerian harmony, bold motivic development, and powerful choral and instrumental combinations, together with the devoutness, restraint, poignancy, and austere power of the highest era of Italian Renaissance polyphony. It was keenly received by the Cecilian Movement, who saw in it a realization of their aim of reviving a Palestrinian a cappella style of church music to counter the secular and worldly tones that customarily accompanied mid-nineteenth-century sacred music. Bruckner's Mass is closest to the style of sixteenth-century vocal counterpoint in the Kyrie (which is in effect an a cappella movement, as the instrumental parts are optional) and the Sanctus. The latter is polyphony of consummate mastery, beginning with an eight-part

[2] See Howie, 'Traditional and Novel Elements in Bruckner's Sacred Music'.

canonic structure, based on a motif from Palestrina's Missa Brevis (where it appears at the words 'rex facta'). At bar 27 the brass enter to crown the words 'Dominus Deus Sabaoth', which are powerfully and majestically announced on repeated *fff* chords. The cadence, to the words 'in excelsis', climbing to G major with the power of an apocalyptic vision, is coloured with the telling sonorous dissonances which enrich the harmony of the whole work from the third bar of the Kyrie onwards. Bruckner specially noted on his manuscript that both the Kyrie and Sanctus were to be conducted in 4/4, thus ensuring their effect of unhurried dignity and awe.

No other Catholic church music of the Romantic era (with the exception perhaps of Liszt's late *Via Crucis*) combines intense expressiveness with such simplicity of means; the work foreshadows an almost twentieth-century concept of vocal and instrumental texture and intimate harmonic subtlety. The reserving of the words 'Gloria in excelsis Deo' and 'Credo in unum Deum' for plainsong intonation implies that Bruckner was thinking foremost of liturgical use for this Mass. Indeed the comparatively severe texture of the several a cappella sections gives it a firmer liturgical atmosphere than the Masses in D minor and F minor. However, the work would serve admirably in either liturgical or concert performance.

The mood and context of the text of each section of the Mass, as always, predestine Bruckner's musical response. Compare the firm homophonic movement of such a passage as 'Et resurrexit' from the Credo with the intense pleading of the contrapuntal 'miserere' from the Agnus Dei, with its anguished, widely leaping bass part. Sonata form is strictly followed in the Benedictus, yet the richness of the chromatic harmony is Bruckner's direct and characteristic emotional response to the words. The opening of the Kyrie is in the Phrygian mode, with chords hovering above a tonic pedal and expressively powerful crescendos leading to the more intense and contrapuntal 'Christe'. An example of a forthright use of counterpoint is found in the last section of the Gloria, a double fugue (Ex. 13). The animated outer sections of the Credo flank an intimate 'adagio' which emphasizes with particular poignancy the words 'et homo factus est' and 'crucifixus'. The Phrygian close of the Kyrie is reiterated at the close of the whole work in a richer and transcended form, in the final 'dona nobis pacem'. This plea for peace sums up the whole ethos of a work in which, as Nowak has said, 'music becomes prayer'.

Many other memorable passages could be discussed at length, such as the rich key-changes that heighten the meaning of the text in the Gloria, the 'et resurrexit' section of the Credo, where the repeated chords rise up like energy reborn, and the cries of 'miserere' in the Agnus Dei which stand like great Gothic arches, but a whole chapter would fail to do justice to this remarkable Mass. It is significant that in this work Bruckner

Ex. 13

consciously finds the roots of his inspiration in the Renaissance and yet creates music that more than any other work of the 1860s reveals his true personality.

The Cecilian Movement which welcomed the Mass in E minor was founded by Franz Xaver Witt. He strove for the total exclusion of the orchestra from devotional music of the Roman Catholic Church, and so did not approve of Bruckner's Masses in D minor and F minor. Both Bruckner and Liszt ultimately turned aside from the Cecilian Movement because of its extreme Palestrinianism. The E minor Mass is a perfect illustration of how far Bruckner was prepared to go in this direction without sacrificing his personal style. But he did write some strictly modal smaller sacred works including a Phrygian hymn 'Iam lucis' and a Phrygian 'Pange lingua', both of 1868. Witt published the 'Pange lingua' in 1885 but greatly annoyed Bruckner by 'correcting' some of the most poignant dissonances. A Lydian gradual 'Os justi' dates from 1879, dedicated to another arch-Cecilianist, Ignaz Traumihler of St Florian. Bruckner wrote to him: 'I should be very pleased if you found pleasure in the piece. It is written without sharps and flats, without the chord of the seventh, without six-four chord and without chordal combinations of four and five simultaneous notes.'[3] Despite the severity of these

---

[3] Letter of 25 July 1879.

restrictions, this motet is profoundly emotional in effect, the contrapuntal main section being introduced by a homophonic passage including antiphonal responses between the male and female voices of the choir, and a plainsong Alleluia closes the work.

The Mass in F minor followed Bruckner's period of personal and professional crisis in 1867 and was completed in the following year. It is his thanksgiving to God for his return to mental and spiritual health. He revised it several times until 1881, when it took on its authentic form. A later revision of 1890–3 was undertaken with Joseph Schalk. Leopold Nowak's edition incorporates changes of orchestration which Bruckner made in 1890–3, though Robert Haas believed that this version contains many unauthorized changes and his edition is based on the original autograph and the revision of 1881. As in the previous Masses, there are many themes influenced by plainsong, notably the first themes of the Gloria and Credo and the 'Pleni sunt coeli' of the Sanctus. The work opens with a step-wise descending motif of four notes in the strings which is taken up by the voices, the basses having an inversion of the motif. Descending groups of four consecutive notes propel much of the Gloria, and they pervade much of the Agnus Dei. In the 'Christe eleison' soprano and bass soloists join the chorus and a solo violin hovers above with an effect reminiscent of the Benedictus of Beethoven's Missa Solemnis. The second Kyrie has a new accompaniment and moves to fresh keys: D flat, followed by a climax on a six-four chord of E major and a final climax, again with soprano and bass soloists in C flat (enharmonic B major) and the chorus turn through C and G flat major back to the home key in the first, and therefore most effective, unaccompanied passage of the Mass—a moment that reappears in Symphony No. 2. Both the Gloria and the Credo, which together form a highly dramatic centrepiece, are in a jubilant C major, close in key and joyful mood to the Te Deum and Psalm 150. Another link with these works occurs in the 'Et resurrexit' section, where an exuberant string motif forms an accompaniment for 101 bars. It is of the same persistent character as the important figures in the Te Deum, Psalm 150, and the sketch of the finale of Symphony No. 9 (Ex. 14).

The central 'Qui tollis peccata mundi' section of the Gloria is in slower tempo in D minor, and its more contrapuntal character contrasts well with the homophonic outer sections. The Gloria ends with a triumphant double fugue to the words 'In gloria Dei Patris' and 'Amen', and involves multiple strettos and inversion. The movement closes with a mighty plagal cadence. The Credo contains some vividly colourful writing, for example the play between fortissimo chorus and pianissimo soloists at 'Deum de Deo', or the violin, viola, and tenor solo parts in the E major 'Et incarnatus'. This movement also ends with a double fugue of astonishing power. Its main subject is derived from the opening theme of the Credo, and the flow of polyphony is punctuated by bold

Ex. 14

cries of 'Credo! Credo!' (Ex. 15). The figure (*x*) in the Credo theme is an ascending form of the opening four-note motif of the Mass, but this does not become clear until the end of the 'Dona nobis pacem'.

Ex. 15

The Sanctus, in F major, quotes the 'Christe' of the opening movement, and the soprano soloist opens the Hosanna in a bright D major.
The Bendictus has a seventeen-bar string prelude which shares the thematic material of the first entry of the soloists. The second theme is sung
by the bass soloist with answering phrases from the sopranos and altos
of the chorus. There is an instrumental link between the A flat major of
the Benedictus and the reprise of the Hosanna in D major. The opening
string motif of the eight-bar prelude to the Agnus Dei, which contains
the descending four-note idea, forms a counterpoint to the choral entry.
In the 'Dona nobis pacem' the Kyrie material reappears, and towards
the end there is a fortissimo statement of the 'Amen' fugue-subject of the
Gloria; this is followed by the Credo theme in augmentation, and now
the relation of this theme to the opening motif of the Mass is made clear.
This descending motif from the first bar of the Kyrie brings Bruckner's
greatest symphonic festive Mass to a gentle close.

The C major gradual 'Locus iste' of 1869 is magically simple and
effective and contains more than a hint of the priests' chorus from *The
Magic Flute*. The opening is hauntingly beautiful (Ex. 16). The gradual

Ex. 16

is in ABA form with homophonic outer parts enclosing an imitative central section which has a climax on B major. The return of Ex. 16 is
smoothly achieved. The later motets of Bruckner are unjustly neglected
and yet none of them presents major problems for a competent choir.
An exploration of this little-known aspect of Bruckner's output brings
exquisite rewards—there are no rivals to works like the austerely beautiful 'Tota pulchra es Maria' (1878), 'Christus factus est' (four-part
setting, 1884), 'Virga Jesse floruit' (1885), or 'Vexilla regis' (1892) among

the output of all Bruckner's contemporaries. 'Ecce sacerdos', with organ and trombones, is the boldest of these works. It is a model example of Bruckner's homophonic choral writing at its finest, his contrapuntal mastery, his use of brass instruments to emphasize the text, his use of material based on plainsong and his extraordinary harmonic daring (for example the climactic sequence of unrelated chords at 'Ideo jure-jurando'). The work was written to celebrate the hundredth anniversary of the Diocese of Linz in 1885.

There are only two major choral works of the Vienna period. The first of these, the Te Deum, completed in 1884, may justifiably be called Bruckner's greatest choral work. Dedicated to his 'dear Lord', it is a gigantic hymn of praise that sums up the composer's rock-like personal faith. The key is C major for strident arpeggio figures (see Ex. 14) and tutti outbursts of brass and chorus that alternate with moments of hushed awe. But there are passages of warmth and beauty which throw these outbursts into splendid relief, such as the two sections in F minor for soloists, 'Tu ergo' and 'Salvum fac'. A solo violin finds voice in these sections and appears in a similar role in the central section of Psalm 150. The various sections of the Te Deum are thematically linked. The soloists prepare for the vast double fugue that ends the work, with 'In te, Domine, speravi', and this is joined by the 'Non confundar in aeternum' theme. The two are then contrapuntally interwoven in a shattering climax that reveals Bruckner's spiritual strength as well as his consummate mastery of technique.

Psalm 150 of 1892, Bruckner's last sacred choral work, shares both the key and the triumphant mood of rapturous exaltation of the Te Deum. Like the earlier work, it uses themes inspired by plainsong and is scored for a full orchestra and chorus, but with only one soprano solo. In some respects it is even bolder, not just through its daring harmonies and choral virtuosity, but by achieving a structural unity and terse compactness, perhaps a result of its exclusion of any elements that might have found more room for expansion in a symphony. The Psalm also ends with a complex fugue, which swiftly builds up to a victorious peroration. It is, like the Te Deum, a personal statement of faith, 'charged with the grandeur of God'.

14

The symphonies in major keys

Perhaps if Wagner had first perused the score of Bruckner's Fourth Symphony in E flat major, rather than his Third, then the composer's Bayreuth nickname might have been 'Bruckner the Horn', rather than 'The Trumpet'. The horns play a memorable part throughout the symphony, notably at statements of the principal themes of both outer movements and throughout much of the Andante, and not unnaturally they preside over the events of the 'Hunt' Scherzo. This captivating use of the horns, poetically evident at the very outset of the work (see Ex. 3, p. 68) is justification enough for Bruckner's own sub-title to this symphony, 'The Romantic'. It is his only use of a descriptive subtitle and, while it is not inappropriate, it should not mislead the listener into an expectation of any features normally associated with nineteenth-century romantic ideology.

The version discussed in this chapter (to which the bar numbers refer) is the revision of 1878/1880, as published by Robert Haas (1936) and by Leopold Nowak in the New Complete Edition (Vol. IV/2, 1953). Bruckner's first version of the symphony, in 1874, contains long passages of exceptional assurance, but the revisions of the first two movements four years later display an altogether more masterly sense of proportion, a general clarity, and the finer handling of climaxes. The third movement was entirely replaced in 1878; again a huge improvement on the galumphing Scherzo and rather thinly inspired Trio of 1874. The fourth movement was to cause Bruckner the most difficulty. In 1878 he shortened it considerably, and then expanded it somewhat in 1880—the form that may be regarded as his final intentions. The opening bars have a warmth, solemn breadth, and unhurried dignity, enhanced by the use of major tonality, that instantly mark the first movement as the most perfect yet conceived by Bruckner. For an entire decade all his large-scale works were written in major keys, from the Fourth Symphony, written in 1874, through the Fifth, Sixth, and Seventh Symphonies and String Quintet to the Te Deum of 1884. This is an especially striking feature when it is recalled that the previous five symphonies and all the main sacred choral works shared minor tonality. The major-key symphonies also share a somewhat less tangible quality, namely a pervading mood of creative confidence. With the 1878/80 version of the Fourth Symphony Bruckner overcame most of the weaknesses which had continued to bedevil him in the revisions of the Third, and the very fact that Symphonies 5, 6, and 7 (and also the Quintet and Te Deum) were hardly revised at all shows that they sprang from an untroubled and confident state of mind, hardly paralleled at any other point in Bruckner's career. In the light of all this the majestic glow of the opening subject of Symphony No. 4 has all the more wonder, and signals with hushed awe the start of an enchanting sequence of transformations that Ex. 3 will undergo, such as the new harmonic lights that appear from bar 12, the ever-varying accompaniment and counterpoints to the theme (see the openings of the development, bar 193, recapitulation, bar 365, and coda, bar 501) and most powerfully of all when its rhythm is used as a chorale towards the end of the development (bar 305).

This movement is a sonata structure, and can be discussed in sonata terms. In both outer movements of Symphony No. 3 Bruckner realized he was struggling with an entirely new formal conception which ran against the grain of sonata form and which, in his revisions, led to serious weaknesses, most importantly the forestalling of the recapitulatory climax with a massive statement of the opening theme in the tonic key in the development. The first movement of Symphony No. 4 does not attempt to solve any of the specific problems addressed in No. 3. Rather it seems Bruckner realized that he had more to say within a more orthodox structure before he was ready to wrestle successfully with a new concept. However, even the fairly inexperienced Bruckernite should not expect a sonata movement in the classical sense of the term. The time-scale and breadth of ideas will be different, and the key-relations and development of motifs will be distinctly unclassical. The opening subject is indeed broad—a seventy-four-bar span, of which the second part is a powerful theme in the home key using the mixed Bruckner rhythm. There is no immediate restatement of this material (as there is in the first groups of Symphonies 3, 6, 7, and 8) but instead a grand formal cadence in the dominant of B flat. The obvious nature of this cadential gesture is too great for all but the most unwary listener to expect that Bruckner will actually begin his second subject in the academically 'correct' key of B flat, and the new idea enters in a spontaneous D flat major. In the recapitulation the same relationship of keys is kept—the cadence on the dominant of A flat heralding the second theme in B major (bar 437). The Coda, propelled by ostinato quaver figures, is given new harmonic life by the introduction of C minor, an obvious enough key for an E flat major movement, and yet almost entirely avoided for 500 bars until this point.

The Andante is a march, funereal and restrained. Its opening paragraph never strays far from C minor, although C flat major is more than once suggested, and it contains three expansive ideas (Ex. 17). The dot-

Ex. 17

(a)

(b)

(c)

ted rhythm (*x*) is an important linking phrase and (b) is a solemn chorale theme. The whole section ends in C major and is followed by a development of (a), with new figures momentarily revealing a vein of suppressed gaiety and moving from C flat major through a wider spectrum of keys. C minor returns for a re-statement of (a) and (c), the latter beginning in D minor and closing in D major. The Coda in C minor (bar 193) is built up using (a) with new semiquaver figures and reaches a mighty C major climax, which glances once more towards C flat major before relaxing quietly with drum taps and hints of phrases of (b) and (c). The effect of the whole movement is almost statuesque, the quiet dignity of the opening C minor never having been ruffled during the modestly solemn procession.

Over a string tremolando hunting horns announce the main idea of the Scherzo. The key is B flat major and the rhythm characteristic:

Ex. 18

A crescendo soon mounts, with dissonances piled up over a tonic pedal. This is resolved unexpectedly by a fortissimo phrase in G flat for horns, trombones, and tuba, answered brightly by trumpets in B flat major. The Bruckner rhythm continues to predominate in the succeeding string phrase, which answers this outburst with a figure neatly derived from it. A crescendo over a dominant pedal in F ensues. The exposition ends with resounding triplet chords for full woodwind, and the development steals in reflectively a semitone higher in G flat major, which is also the key of the Trio. This is the most warmly benign of his Ländler (Ex. 19). Its easeful comfort is gently roused to some curious harmonic travels in its short central development.

Ex. 19

It can well be argued that Bruckner had written nothing finer than the first three movements of this symphony. Unfortunately the Finale runs aground more than once and he has not yet the skill to refloat it. His stream of thought is about to flow into a broad and magnificent sweep but in this Finale a last stretch of rocks and rapids has to be encountered. To stretch the analogy a little further, these rocks and rapids are the vestiges of sonata form which the composer has not yet been able to discard. They impede his natural flow of thought and destroy the momentum of the music. The recapitulation is the stumbling point in the movement: it appears as in sonata form and yet its character and the breadth of its conception demand an altogether different treatment, the kind of treatment that Bruckner perfected in Symphonies 5 and 8, works whose Finales, although quite different, are a perfect foil to the previous three movements. In the Fourth Symphony Finale the weakest element is the second thematic group. This begins promisingly (bar 93) but soon sinks into banality, trite melody and irritatingly repetitive one- and two-bar phrases. Each time this material rears its head it seems more tired and threadbare, particularly throughout the development, which, after a promising start, is interrupted by the second-group material dressed up as a chorale.

The weakness of this section is all the more regrettable in view of the magnificent and totally different opening subject-matter. The movement begins mysteriously in B flat minor over an ostinato, and a crescendo blazes up, with the rhythm of the Scherzo playing an important part, and spills over into the home key with the main subject (Ex. 20).

Ex. 20

The Bruckner rhythm appears in crotchet and minim values in this theme, and the figure (x) becomes one of the most important and effective elements in succeeding tutti passages. Whenever the mood of this opening subject returns, Bruckner rivets the attention, despite the lapses that occur in between, and the coda particularly is engineered with infallible logic and finality. Had the mood of the second subject permeated the coda, then the result might have been a bombastic peroration. Instead there is a crescendo of great dignity and a final blaze of E flat major with trombones and tuba reiterating the rhythm of Ex. 3 (p. 68). The whole symphony is unified not only by several recollections of the rhythm of the opening theme (and its literal quotation at bar 79 of the Finale) but also by subtle thematic integration such as the use of the Bruckner rhythm in the first, third, and fourth movements, the drop of the fifth in the first themes of the first two movements and similar treatments of the fourth and fifth in the Scherzo. (There is also a similarity of mood between passages of the Andante and the Finale—compare bars 101 fol. of the Andante with bars 269 fol. of the Finale.)

The Fifth Symphony—his greatest, most integrated, and arguably most visionary to date—was, ironically, the only one of his numbered and completed symphonies of which he was never to hear a note played. Bruckner was clearly and demonstrably self-assured in the composition of this huge B flat major canvas, a creative confidence evident both to the ear and in the circumstances of its writing. Begun only two months after completing the Fourth, it was finished before he had heard either the Third or the Fourth, and despite the rejection of those two works by Dessoff, the conductor of the Vienna Philharmonic. Also, for a work on this scale and exploring uncharted new realms, the Fifth was sketched in the relatively short space of fifteen months, despite Bruckner's busy teaching life and organ playing in Vienna. It was written with a sure and lively hand.

The opening is a single strand of sound—a low pizzicato ostinato—above which a mighty contrapuntal span is steadily foretold: the tempo is adagio. (These introductory bars are heard again at the Finale's opening.) The brass enter with two huge chorale-like statements, each followed by a dramatic pause. Then the strings quicken the tempo and again the texture is linear, contrapuntal. These polyphonic preludes to the drama will ultimately coalesce in the mighty 'fugal-sonata' form of the Finale. After another massive chordal preparation, on what seems to be the dominant of D minor, the Allegro gets under way. The apparent dominant (A) falls to D, which takes its place as part of a B flat major chord (Ex. 21). Symphony No. 5 thus at once surprises and perplexes by

Ex. 21

its breaking down of all previously preconceived patterns. After fifty bars elaborating and developing Ex. 21, three further substantial and clearly contrasted ideas can be discerned before the pizzicato figures of the slow introduction return. When the lively tempo resumes, following this mid-way oasis, the themes are subjected to an ever more complex array of contrapuntal devices (canon, inversion, diminution, etc.) in a constant process of re-inventive development. A falling octave idea (which introduced itself as early as bar 63) becomes growingly significant, and is another important link with the Finale, as is the increasingly luminous chorale motif. The four main thematic groups are restated in new harmonic lights, varied textures and continued transformation (not so much recapitulation as redevelopment). In the last bars the brass turn Ex. 21 into a triumphant fanfare—the unquenchable B flat major form in which it will return at the end of the symphony.

Another pizzicato accompaniment announces the Adagio. Its 6/4 rhythm is set starkly against the 4/4 melody that joins it on the oboe.

The key of D minor, and the series of falling sevenths that are added to the sad procession, create a mood of wistful nostalgia. In wonderful contrast, a glow of consoling warmth surges forth with the next string theme (in C major), which is contrapuntally developed through various bright keys. Labelling these two sections A and B, the shape of the entire movement can be summarized prosaically as ABABA. But this says nothing about the successively beguiling richness that is added as each paragraph returns. The last A section is akin to a gigantic coda, with new and enchanting ornamentations smoothing out the original stark cross-rhythms. Pizzicato falling sevenths turn quietly at the close to a subdued, inconclusive D major.

Just as the outer movements are linked, so are the inner ones. The Scherzo is ushered in with a fast statement of the accompaniment figure that opened the slow movement (and in the same key); later there are patterns of familiar falling sevenths. A delicious Ländler occasionally interrupts the fun and flurry, until all is swept away in a dazzle of D major. A horn seems to insist that the Trio should be in G flat (F sharp) rather than the B flat major of the key signature. The Trio is a scene of lively rustic charm, sketched with delicate and restrained strokes; as so often, it is the perfect dramatic counterpoise to the insistent Scherzo figures.

Thematic unity (which Bruckner had striven for in the Fourth Symphony) is manifestly a feature of Symphony No. 5, but the techniques employed in its Finale are strikingly different from those in any other Bruckner symphony and the movement is so significant that a fairly detailed thematic analysis proves richly rewarding. The opening section consists of reminiscences of the previous movements, but while these might outwardly suggest the influence of Beethoven's Ninth, the effect and purpose of this set of thematic recollections are quite different. First to appear is the growing string counterpoint over the pizzicato bass tread from the slow introduction to the opening movement, with the significant addition of a falling octave-figure from the clarinet. There is a pause and the clarinet octave-figure appears stark and alone, now extended to become the motto figure of the entire movement. Next follows the main theme of the opening movement (appearing exactly as in bars 55 to 62 of the first movement, Ex. 21), but again with the addition of falling octaves from clarinet followed by trumpet. The motto theme once more appears questioningly and arrestingly, and then the oboe theme that opened the Adagio makes its entry accompanied by the pizzicato triplet string figures that linked the Adagio and the Scherzo. Again the motto figure sounds—now on two clarinets—and is taken up by the cellos and basses and extended to form the first fugue subject (Ex. 22). This section is a grand march-like fugal exposition (bars 31–66), the tutti dying away on the home dominant and leading to a non-fugal 'second subject' in D flat major. This new group, which is in graceful contrast

Ex. 22

to the fugal material, flows through brighter keys but also ends on the home dominant (bar 136). A tutti follows, based on the motto figure in augmentation and in its original form, with scale figures in the strings which take their cue from the second subject. The exposition ends with a great chorale, stated antiphonally by resounding brass and quiet strings (Ex. 23).

Ex. 23

This final paragraph moves from G flat major to a quiet F major (the home dominant again—a Neapolitan relationship) and after a few moments' reflection on the chorale melody, a second fugal exposition begins with this very theme as subject (bar 223). Soon both fugue-subjects (Exx. 22 and 23) are combined (bar 270) and a massive development ensues in which they are freely interwoven and inverted. The effect is that of a grand and vastly extended symphonic tutti. The detailed progress of the two subjects is best left undescribed as it provides a source of constant wonder at every hearing. The climax comes with a mighty statement of the two subjects combined, preceded by a crescendo (bar 374)—a moment that has the feel of a recapitulatory climax, but such terminology is redundant in any attempt to map the mighty swing of Bruckner's creative process in this particular movement. The second subject follows, with subtle transformations, in F major. As before, a tutti section ensues, but the principal subject of the first movement (Ex. 21) now joins in to play a conspicuous role. The Coda (bar 496) has a breadth and grandeur which are unparalleled in Bruckner's output. It begins quietly with scale-patterns and the motto figure, soon combined with the theme from the first movement. The climax of the whole movement is achieved when the motto figure appears in augmentation, both in its original form and in inversion, and then forms a background to the chorale which blazes forth resplendently in the brass. The main theme of the opening movement ends this Finale in which Bruckner seems to link heaven and earth in one immutable visionary span. With it is the final proof of his awakened mastery, and the enemy's jeers are left far, far behind.

Strangely, the Bruckner rhythm plays virtually no part in the Fifth Symphony, whereas it dominated most of the Fourth. In Symphony No. 6 in A major it becomes a driving force which is predominant from the outset (see Ex. 24). The metrical complexities caused by this rhythm

Ex. 24

(including combined statements in different note values) are more marked in the first movement of the Sixth Symphony than in any other work and this may be a factor in the strange neglect that the work has suffered. As with Symphony No. 5, Bruckner never heard a complete performance of it, nor was it published until after his death. His own opinion was: 'The Sixth is the cheekiest'. The rarity of its performance is all the more surprising in view of its bright character and key, and its abundance of warm and memorable themes.

The foreign notes, G natural, B flat, and F natural, in Ex. 24 are characteristic Neapolitan elements and they foreshadow several Neapolitan relationships which follow. The theme extends over twenty bars or so, accompanied throughout by the rhythm (*x*), and incorporates an important motif (Ex. 25). There is a tutti counterstatement. As the develop-

Ex. 25

mf cresc.

ment gathers energy, freely inverted statements of Exx. 24 and 25 reveal the glorious richness of Bruckner's melodic imagination in a particular way unique to this symphony. This development is propelled throughout by the triplet figures which first made their appearance during the third subject of the exposition. Similarly at the end of the movement they flow into the coda (bar 309) and glide alongside serene reflections of Ex. 24. The rhythm (*x*) returns for the last tutti statement, which is a vast plagal cadence based on Ex. 24. A word must be added about the approach to the recapitulation, which in some ways foreshadows the first movement of Symphony No. 8. During the development of Ex. 25 the tempo quickens, and Ex. 24, together with its accompanying rhythmic figure (*x*), appears in fullest splendour in E flat major—the polar opposite of the home key, A major. Immediately it is restated in G flat, then again in A flat which becomes the home dominant and the whole first subject appears *fff* in the tonic, followed this time by a quiet counterstatement (the opposite procedure to the exposition). This approach to the recapitulation is arresting, dramatic, and truly climactic.

Tovey rightly remarked that the F major Adagio of this symphony has 'a high order of solemn beauty'.[1] It is cast in colossal but clear sonata form and is the only example in the symphonies of a sonata structure Adagio. The elegiac oboe addition to the main theme (bar 5 of Ex. 26) is related to the rhythm of Ex. 25 from the first movement. More significantly this idea occurs again in the Finale (bar 130), in the course of which movement its relation to Ex. 25 becomes clear.

Bruckner's scherzos are by no means all alike: their differences are much more striking than their similarities. The example from Symphony No. 6 inhabits an enchanted world all of its own. The tempo is slower than usual and the key A minor. A captivating feature is Bruckner's avoidance of a root-position tonic chord for the first hundred bars of this Scherzo: A major is only grasped firmly in the final few tutti bars. The Trio is a dialogue between pizzicato strings, three horns, and woodwind. The key is C major, though this seems to be a point for debate: the string chords pointing towards D flat major and the woodwind quot-

---

[1] *Essays in Musical Analysis: Symphonies and other Orchestral Works* (Oxford, 1981), p. 263.

Ex. 26

ing the main theme of Symphony No. 5 in A flat major, turning it upside down at the last appearance. This Trio is utterly unlike that of any other Bruckner symphony.

If the myth of the stereotyped Bruckner symphony still needs exploding, then a comparison between the Finale of this symphony and that of its mighty predecessor is recommended. This Finale is a steady, organic assertion of A major against or, if you like, via its Neapolitan relatives (those 'foreign' notes, with their own implied tonalities, that feature in Ex. 24). The movement opens in A minor, or more accurately, its first idea is in the Phrygian mode, with the note F leading off disconsolately over a tremolo E pedal. The strong idea in the brass at bar 37 emphasizes F again, and also B flat. The C major *Gesangsperiode* stresses the note G. Contrary to some recorded interpretations it may be noted that the characteristic marking 'Bewegt, doch nicht zu schnell' (not too fast) does *not* slow further at this point. The goal of this difficult but supremely rewarding movement is the crowning in the last bars of Ex. 24 in A major. The battle being fought is akin to that engaged in the Finale to Symphony No. 4. The unique Finale to No. 5 was a heroic enterprise of another order. The victorious conclusion of Bruckner's quest for a new and ideal finale form will be celebrated in that to

No. 8. The Sixth Symphony's development is an eminent and profoundly satisfying landmark on that triumphant march.

The work which brought to Bruckner the fullest measure of success and the greatest joy in his lifetime was Symphony No. 7 in E major. It was his turning point towards an international reputation. Today it remains the most readily accessible and strikingly beautiful of his symphonies. Of them all, the Seventh has had the easiest passage and has enjoyed the greatest popularity. Ludwig II of Bavaria accepted the dedication and so allowed his name to grace the title page, a dizzying honour for Bruckner who had the royal title emblazoned above his own name (which appeared in tiny letters) in a style, as Erwin Doernberg noted, 'which a Byzantine emperor might have deemed overpolite'.[2] The orchestra, with its quartet of Wagner tubas, is the largest he had yet called for; but it is not huge, and is mainly used with economy to produce (especially in the brass) a variety of glimmerings and sonorous effects. Above all in this symphony it is the strings who propel much of the broad sweep of song-like melody: lyrical lines of woodwind follow in intricate tracery.

The cellos, reinforced by horn, violas, and clarinet, present the opening theme (to a background of tremolo violins) which, beginning with a wide arpeggio, seems to pass through a series of noble, vaulted arches (Ex. 27). A key to the drama of the whole first movement is found here in the early insistence (by the ninth bar in fact) of the dominant key, B major. The solemn arpeggio motif (*a*) of the first three bars of Ex. 27 and the figure (*b*) from bars 10 to 11 are elements of distinct importance throughout the movement. There follows a fully scored counterstatement. With the opening of the tranquil second thematic group (bar 51) we are faced with the Toveyan riddle, 'When is a key not a key?' The opening of the second group is *on* but not *in* the dominant. B major is not yet settled, and at this point there has been no clear modulation to it. However, towards the end of the second group (bar 103) a huge crescendo builds up on the dominant of B and so a new and important third theme enters in B minor (see Ex. 5, page 69). This moment comes as a great release in tension and the pattern of the drama now becomes clear—it is based on the relationship of the tonic key, E major, and the forthright and more firmly established dominant key of B. The exposition ends in B major with lyrical calm.

The succeeding development of the material can be broadly viewed in several sections. The first is concerned with imitative reflections on Ex. 27 in inversion and the second with the main idea of the second group, also in inversion. The third theme follows in E minor accompanied by its own mirror inversion, enhanced with new counterpoints, and settling on the dominant of C. Now enters a mighty statement of Ex. 27 in the

[2] *The Life and Symphonies of Anton Bruckner* (London, 1960).

Ex. 27

key of C minor with grandly resounding imitations from the brass section. There is a counterstatement in D minor which moves towards A flat major but is forestalled by the return of the theme in the home key of E, a truly wonderful entry after the grim darkness of the C minor statement. The second group enters now in E minor, significantly avoiding the dominant, and the third group, which played the most important role in establishing B in the exposition, now enters in the new and surprising key of G. This is the crucial point of the movement—a skilful, quiet, and purposeful avoidance of the establishment of the dominant key. With the coda comes a solemn and noble climax which fully establishes the home key, and E major shines forth in its own right for the first time since Ex. 27 (*a*) opened the movement.

On 22 January 1883, three weeks before Wagner's death, Bruckner began the Adagio. He wrote to Felix Mottl: 'One day I came home and felt very sad. The thought had crossed my mind that before long the Master would die, and then the C sharp minor theme of the Adagio [Ex. 28] came to me.' The first phrase of this most solemn theme is stated by a quartet of Wagner tubas—the first occasion on which Bruckner called for these instruments. The impassioned continuation is declaimed by the strings. Ex. 28 is but the opening span of the theme, which is over thirty bars long. The second main theme is in F sharp major. It is set in a faster 3/4 time, has a characteristic 'off the beat' start, and is truly ravishing (Ex. 29).

Ex. 28

Ex. 29

The span of the movement can be summarized: ABA¹B¹A² Coda. The two themes are thus counterstated each in a richly expanded variation (A¹ and B¹). Their respective tempos and distinct orchestration are retained in both of these statements. A² becomes the great climax of the movement. The tubas carry the opening theme over new accompaniments and, as the tension mounts, the trombones introduce an allusion to the theme that Bruckner uses in his Te Deum at the words 'Non confundar in aeternum', which is treated in sequence. This is a reference of obvious programmatic significance. At the height of the climax the music is poised on the dominant of the home key, C sharp, only to open on to C major at the crucial moment. This is a most wonderful letting-in of the light, which effectively releases the tension of one of Bruckner's finest crescendos and at the same time reserves the radiant glow of the tonic major for the coda. Bruckner was understandably much affected by the news of Wagner's death, and his reaction found its artistic sub-limation in the elevated coda to the movement—sombre music for tubas and horns, ending with a transfigured major version of the opening melody. Bruckner always referred to this passage as 'the funeral music for the Master'.

There has been must discussion of the controversial cymbal clash at the point of climax in this slow movement, which appears in certain edi-tions of the score. I would agree with Robert Simpson's apt comment that Bruckner's climax is quite noble enough to withstand the cymbal crash here, and so it is not a very serious point to dispute. But for the record it ought to be stated that the idea was not Bruckner's own, and this is revealed in a letter of Joseph Schalk to his brother Franz of 10 January 1885: 'Recently I went with Löwe over the score of the Seventh Symphony with regard to some changes and emendations. . . . Perhaps you do not know that Nikisch has insisted on the acceptance of our desired cymbal clash in the Adagio, as also on triangle and timpani, which pleases us immensely.'

The funereal serenity of the Adagio gives way to two movements of the most impassioned confidence and exultation that Bruckner ever wrote. The A minor Scherzo has a wild and playful joy that at moments anticipates Mahler and even Elgar. The section is cast in orthodox sonata form but all the elements of the design are stated in the first twelve bars. Throughout the movement rapid shifts from key to key should be observed, and the development section is rich in strettos, inversions, and many intricate contrapuntal combinations of the several motifs of the movement. The F major Trio, introduced by a rhythm from the Scherzo on the drum, is cast in binary form. A straightforward pastoral melody pervades it, which is inverted at the beginning of the second section. The key of the Trio has a fresh and appealing quality, as it was nowhere found in the Scherzo and only treated as a sequential passing key in the earlier movements. Similarly the A minor of the Scherzo was avoided in the Adagio, and C sharp minor in turn was not used before the slow movement despite its close relationship to the home key of E.

The opening arpeggio theme of the Finale (Ex. 30) is closely related to the opening of the first movement, and at the end of the symphony both themes merge together. The fourth movement is one of grand jubilation, uniting gaiety and grandeur and tackling a new formal conception (only most tentatively related to sonata form) in a way that is different from all the other finales. Once again the essential drama of the music is a tonal struggle, in this case between E major and A flat major. Just as the unexpected incursions of C minor and C major respectively widened the horizons of the first and second movements, so the Finale's structure hangs upon key relations, and they are juxtaposed right at the outset. At the opening, with another string tremolo as background, confident upward-surging figures begin in E major (the very first phrase is not unlike the arpeggio shape of the symphony's opening) but turn to end with a very distinctive cadence in A flat major (Ex. 30). This cadential

Ex. 30

figure always has the function of pulling the music rapidly from one key centre to another. The whole structure can be viewed, tonally, as a grad-ual advance towards an inevitable establishment of the home key of E. There is further expansion of the exuberant opening phrases before the second main idea appears—again a very Brucknerian one—a chorale (marked with a pizzicato bass) centred on A flat. It is sung at its outset by strings, and then the Wagner tubas appear for the first time since the Adagio. The chorale's stately course is roughly interrupted by a colossal unison tutti statement (in A minor), which sounds at first like a third new idea, but is an emphatic development and extension of the buoyant arpeg-gio phrase from the first bars. It climbs, striding dramatically and inex-orably in strong dotted rhythms and halts again with the brusque gesture of a trill. Restated a semitone higher, it then continues with vigorous marching tread through a passage of contrary-motion imitation. The mood is truly grand, with the dotted rhythms resplendent in brass colours (recalling the magnificence of the Finale to the Fifth Symphony) and is extended (mainly by the strings) to further joyous transformations of the opening phrases, and even playful diminuations of the chorale idea.

In their progress, these themes are heard continuously afresh, their development is constant and organic. In this lies one of Bruckner's most magnificent achievements, for the form of his Finale is entirely new in conception. It is another proof of the self-certainty of his creative think-ing that the elements fuse and re-emerge so effortlessly and satisfacto-rily. In the coda, with its triumphant celebration of the Finale's arpeggio figures in E major, the first phrases of the opening movement also return in splendour.

15

The Eighth and Ninth Symphonies

The brightest fortunes of Bruckner's last years were the result of the tremendous success of the Seventh Symphony. Its successor, Symphony No. 8 in C minor, which he regarded as his finest work, caused him the greatest emotional strain of his whole career.

In 1885 Hermann Levi had triumphed with the première of the Seventh Symphony in Munich, which Bruckner attended. He promised to devote his energy to the further establishment of Bruckner's fame, and the delighted composer accepted the conductor as his friend and 'artistic father' and proceeded with his next symphony. The Eighth is a far bigger and more complex work than any of its predecessors: when Levi received the score in 1887 he rejected it in bewilderment (see chapter 6). The shock of his artistic father's reaction plunged Bruckner into an intensive revision of the score, which he completed in 1890. Thus there are two versions of the score, the 1887 original and the 1890 revision. There are many radical differences between these two versions which deserve comment, but first the more familiar version must be examined, that is the 1890 revision. (Bar numbers refer to Nowak's score in Vol. VIII/2 of the complete edition. It must be remembered that Haas incorporated certain elements of the original 1887 version of the work in his edition of the 1890 score. He restored ten bars of the Adagio, and thirty-eight of the Finale which Bruckner had simply excised, probably as a result of Joseph Schalk's persuasion. These restorations are eminently justifiable, and because of them Haas has given us a score that many commentators and conductors have found to make far more musical sense and to have a more convincing formal balance.)

Ambiguous tonality characterizes the opening of the symphony. A violin tremolando on F forms the background to the opening theme in the lower strings. It instantly conveys the impression of a first unit reaching out over what must surely be a mighty span (Ex. 31). This is a daring opening for a symphony in C minor. In fact it begins in what would appear to be B flat minor and turns dramatically to C only at its close. These two keys, B flat minor and C minor, are of crucial significance in the overall structure. Indeed the whole structure can be legitimately viewed as a duel between them. The dotted rhythm of the first three bars

Ex. 31

of the theme is identical to the rhythm of the opening of Beethoven's Ninth, but both its character and the direction of its harmonies are utterly different. The figure (*c*) at the end of the first phrase is found as a cadence figure at various important points in the symphony, particularly at the end of the first movement, in modified form in the coda of the Adagio, and at the close of the entire work where it is reiterated in a C major transformation. The tiny figure (*a*) also plays its own part, often in inversion, and appearing in tense and sinister repetitions. By bar 8, (*b*) of Ex. 31 has grown into a new variant, and the further continuation of the theme shows it growing organically into new shapes. This process is characteristic of the motivic development that all the important themes of the work undergo. As the tremolando rises in chromatic steps, the lower strings embrace the Bruckner rhythm. This rhythm is taken up by all the strings and inverted, and the whole opening idea cadences fleetingly in the home key. Without any pause a fortissimo counterstatement ensues.

Imitative reflections on the Bruckner-rhythm motif extend the close of the counterstatement and lead into the second-subject group (bar 51), which is derived from this very motif. Thus the first- and second-subject groups are organically linked. During the course of the second thematic section the triplet figures of the Bruckner rhythm are to the fore, and so another link is formed, this time to the third-subject group (bar 97), which is permeated throughout by triplet rhythms. In his early minor-key symphonies (and it should be recalled that this is the composer's third C minor symphony) Bruckner modulated to the relative major for his second subject. In the first movement of the Eighth the second subject is in G major, and the relative major, E flat major, is attained only at the very end of the exposition where it is celebrated by a pæan of fanfares (bar 125). This latest idea—the arpeggio fanfare—can be discerned throughout the work as well (notably in the Finale at bars 11 and 25, and in the coda of the Finale after bar 687).

The masterly central section of the movement is one of the most impressive passages in Bruckner's entire output. Broadly viewed, the E flat fanfare passage is followed by a return of the opening theme and the 'development' section enters almost imperceptibly. Inversions of Ex. 31 are the first points of discussion, followed by an appearance of the inverted second subject, set in new and richer tonalities. Then the music settles on the dominant of the home key. This moment is easily recognized. The figure (a) of Ex. 31 is reiterated in the bass while the Bruckner-rhythm motif ascends inexorably in the upper strings. The expectation of a recapitulation in the home key is aroused by this passage, but then figure (a) begins to climb upwards ominously in the bass until it becomes fixed on the dominant of B flat minor—the other element in this great combat of keys. And so the opening idea (in augmentation) is recapitulated in a massive statement in B flat minor, which lifts into C major, with the addition of the Bruckner-rhythm motif in augmentation above. Eight horns celebrate with exuberant dotted rhythms. Then there is a sudden shift into D flat minor and the theme is repeated again, this time opening on E flat major. A third statement follows in the next breath in F minor, which now ends in C minor and the blaze of sound is cut off, leaving a single flute trailing down and the cellos and basses reiterating figure (c) with a disconsolate air. The trumpets announce the rhythm of the opening theme on a monotone of C. The figure (c) is then taken up and used in a swirling passage which leads to a recapitulation of the entire opening theme in C minor, beginning quietly and almost imperceptibly in the oboe (bar 282). This entirely original concept of recapitulation in the form of three huge tonal steps leading to a quiet thematic restatement is engineered in a way that significantly ensures that the home key is not firmly achieved. Thus the tension of the tonal struggle is prolonged.

The C minor Coda is music of profound tragedy. At the height of an overwhelming climax which follows the recapitulation of the third subject group, horns and trumpets repeat the rhythm of Ex. 31 on a stark monotone of C and continue this for four bars after the rest of the orchestra breaks off. Bruckner referred to this moment as 'the annunciation of death'. Drum rolls and shattered fragments (firstly of phrase (b) of Ex. 31) follow, and finally phrase (c) is repeated over and over again until the movement reaches its quiet close (compare Ex. 8, p. 78). This last series of repeated phrases of (a) was referred to as the *Totenuhr* by Bruckner. A man is dying in a room, but a clock in the room ticks on even when his life has passed away.

The motions of a turbulent spirit that overshadow the first movement are released with elemental freedom and boundless energy in the Scherzo, where two combined one-bar phrases are ecstatically repeated. The prevailing keys are C minor and E flat major, and in the final nine bars C major. The Trio (cast like the Scherzo in sonata form) employs harps: their first entry at bar 37 with horns and pizzicato strings is thoroughly Austrian in character. The profound and immense Adagio is in D flat major. By bar 15 there is a grand ascending A major arpeggio idea, crowned with an upward rising turn. This will form the basis for the climax to the whole structure (bar 239). The whole thematic exposition so far is over gently syncopated string chords. The next important idea, beginning in E major but modulating widely, is introduced by the cellos at bar 47. The overall mood of these sections, which now alternate with characteristic elaboration and enrichment of harmony and scoring, is of tension followed by a relaxation of transcendent calm. No late nineteenth-century master other than Bruckner could so effectively hold the helm for almost half an hour of such solemn tension and release as in this Adagio.

Superficially, the Finale has much in common with the first movement, particularly the tonal ambiguity of its opening bars (Ex. 32). The dotted

Ex. 32

rhythm of the first subject, the character of the second group (bar 69), the E flat minor double-unison structure of the third subject (bar 135) and the subsequent establishment of the relative major (E flat) after much suspense. But the specific characters of each of the combined elements—melody, rhythm, harmony, and orchestration—are so different that the effect is rather akin to the sensation of experiencing a beclouded and turbulent night that gives way to a lustrous dawn.

Every symphony of Bruckner's is a structure of imposing size and variety, but none of them culminates in a unitary span of the magnificence achieved in No. 8. The culmination of this unitary span is the combination of themes from all four movements in an exultant celebration of the tonic major (Ex. 33). It is not contrapuntal ingenuity that dazzles us

Ex. 33

here, but rather the power, logic, and inevitability of this final fusion, cast in the simplicity of a C major chord. The symphony which caused Bruckner the greatest personal anxiety thus represents the very essence of achievement. Its content is of aspiration and struggle towards symphonic unity on an unparalleled scale.

To the listener who is well acquainted with the 1890 score an examination of how it differs from the original of 1887 will bring many surprises. These differences provide a fascinating insight into the mind of a great artist engaged in totally recasting his original creative conception. The score and parts of the original version were issued in April 1973 in an edition by Nowak, and the version was first performed by the Bournemouth Symphony Orchestra under Hans-Hubert Schönzeler in a BBC broadcast the following September. The original score is inferior in a great many aspects to the final version, and in a sense Levi's rejection (whatever his reasons for it were) did Bruckner a good turn in the long run. The differences are so many that it is far beyond the scope of this chapter to mention more than an important handful of them, but they apply in every movement to every aspect—melody, rhythm, harmony, and orchestration.

Instantly striking is the re-orchestration. The 1887 score employed two-part woodwind as opposed to the three-part of the revision. (So much for the myth of Bruckner's dependence on huge orchestral forces.) The four Wagner tubas are much busier in the opening movement in the original version, while the harps disappear from the Trio of the Scherzo, and only one harp is called for in the Adagio, as opposed to the 'three if possible' in the revised score. The Adagio asks for piccolo in the original version and the climax is certainly enhanced by its employment. This is the only instance of Bruckner ever scoring for piccolo. The climax of the original Adagio also contrives to contain six cymbal clashes as opposed to the two in the revision.

The differences of form and tonality between the two scores are the most significant of all and reveal most clearly the benefits of the revision. They are apparent from the outset. It will be recalled that this symphony, in C minor, begins in fact in B flat minor and reaches the home key only at the end of its dramatic first thematic phrase. In the familiar revised version a clarinet figure reinforces C minor when it is achieved, thus confirming the tonality (see Ex. 31). In the original score this figure does not appear. A more important alteration to the first movement is the total overhauling of the approach to the recapitulation, the recapitulation itself and the counterstatement of the opening theme in the recapitulation. This entire central section is vastly superior in the revised score, the original revealing that Bruckner had not properly worked out his ideas, and the sense of the conflict of keys is missing in the earlier score, where the logic of the tonality is lost and the orchestration much less effective. The whole passage benefits in the revision by being shortened. The most noticeable difference in the opening movement, however, is the Coda. The revised version ends tragically and quietly with repetitions of (c) from Ex. 31, and is the only outer movement of all Bruckner's symphonies not to end fortissimo. The original, on the other hand, continues after a pause for another thirty bars with a tutti peroration which is based on a double augmentation of Ex. 31, passing from B flat minor (harmonized as G flat major, starting at letter Z) to a triumphant C major. The passage is very effective, but despite this Bruckner was right to discard it, as it forestalls the C major ending of the symphony and thus weakens the overall tonal pattern.

The original Scherzo and Finale are essentially the same as in the revision (aside from countless tiny alterations), except that they were both originally longer. The Scherzo of the original is inferior in a number of small details and is even more obsessed with the principal motif. The Finale of the original contained brass lines at the opening of the Coda and delightful pianissimo trumpet fanfares just before the final C major tutti. Both these elements were deleted in the revision. The close of the whole symphony differs also in that the great unison statement of the motif derived from (c) of Ex. 31 is missing in the original.

A further word should be said about the Trio of the second movement and the Adagio, both of which were considerably altered. The entire first theme of the Trio is quite different in the original, the important triplet fanfares for trumpets appear as duplets and many other details are strangely different. The climax of the Adagio is longer, orchestrated differently and considerably inferior in the earlier version, but its most striking feature is that the climax comes in C major as opposed to E flat major. There are several possible explanations of this important change. Bruckner may have felt that he should not have this climax in the same key as the Adagio of his previous symphony (the Adagio of No. 7 also culminates in C at its climax). More important, it would seem that he felt (as with the coda to the first movement) that C major must be avoided and kept out of play until the close of the entire drama.

With Symphony No. 9 in D minor Bruckner's range of expression was widened and the visionary quality of his mature style intensified. The first ninety-six bars of the opening movement contain eight principal ideas. The first, Ex. 34(a) below, is a reminiscence of the opening of his Missa Solemnis, composed when he was only thirty. Ex. 34(b) contains many elements that will be familiar: the fifths and octaves and arpeggio figures, as well as the extraordinarily wide span. There are more things of heaven and earth in this gigantic statement than were ever dreamt of in any other first-subject group (Ex. 34). The form of the movement

Ex. 34

Ex. 34 *cont.*

clearly shows a pattern of 'Statement, Counterstatement and Coda' which is totally divorced from sonata form. Indeed the solemn and broad scope of the first section indicates that quite a different concept lies ahead. The second principal section of the Statement is a slower theme beginning in A major (bar 97), and the third section consists of two main ideas in Moderato tempo (the first beginning in D minor, bar 167, and the second beginning in G flat major, bar 191).

The Counterstatement (bar 227) begins with stretto treatments of Ex. 34(a) followed by a glowing appearance of (b). Then (a) and (c) are treated in combination, leading to a still grander appearance of (b). There is a pause and the second idea from the third section enters with pizzicato accompaniment. The first-section material continues after this, first with (c), joined shortly by (d) and (e) together. An accelerando and crescendo lead to the climax of the Counterstatement—a D minor *fff* statement of (f), which proceeds to step forward in new lights and through a series of massive tonal shifts. The second and third sections are in due turn counterstated (bars 421 and 459 respectively) and the Coda (bar 517) returns to ideas from Ex. 34, namely fragments of (b) and (f) and a statement in augmentation of (g) which has not been heard since the original Statement.

The above is the broadest survey of this colossal structure and it takes little or no account of either tonality or the character and interrelationships of themes. It should be stressed that both the Counterstatement and Coda represent one continuous and constant process of development.

Foremost amongst the very apparent features of the Ninth Symphony is its advanced harmonic language. The end of the first movement is a clear example of forthright dissonance—a grinding of simultaneous tonic and flat supertonic harmony. In the strangely troubled world of the D minor Scherzo one particular and unmistakable discord, (*x*) of Ex. 35, is in evidence in one form or another throughout the entire movement.

Ex. 35

In the spectral Trio 'on horror's head horrors accumulate'. The harmony is at times scarcely definable, for example at the opening of the E major Adagio which has already been mentioned (see Ex. 1, p. 65). The wide leap of the ninth at the outset of the Adagio points forward to Schoenberg, while other ecstatic melodic leaps during the same movement anticipate Mahler.

At bar 29 of the slow movement appears a sadly descending chorale in the choir of horns. The composer referred to this as his 'farewell to life'. The second main thematic group of the Adagio begins in the violins at bar 45, with a characteristic 'off-the-beat' lift at the start. It is with the recapitulation of this theme that Bruckner builds to the movement's climax. The latter is achieved with an unexpected, vast, and terrifying restatement of the first phrase of Ex. 1 surrounded with the harshest possible dissonance. This dreadful vision is then dispelled as the closing E major is re-established and valedictory images from the Miserere of the D minor Mass, the Adagio of the Eighth, and the opening theme of the Seventh Symphony greet our ears.

The unfinished Finale occupied Bruckner for the last two years of his life. There exist no fewer than six variants of the movement in sketched full score. These sketches show that the finale was planned on a scale more ambitious than that of the Eighth Symphony or even of the Fifth. The published editions of the sketches reveal, at least in outline, a gigantic structure consisting of an exposition followed by a development combining a fugue with a recapitulation of the second-subject group. Thus the characteristic tendency of Bruckner's late years towards telescoping development and recapitulation can be observed. But the movement is incomplete and is not completable. Much detail of the inner parts, the sense of coherent continuity and the entire Coda are missing, and none but the composer himself could supply such elements. Bruckner simply did not live long enough to envisage this finale as a truly unified entity.

What remains is a torso representing the composer's faithfully recorded final visions; visions which were abruptly ended and not left to the world in a tangible enough form to allow performance or even speculative completion.

It is, however, no mean fragment. The complete sketches, 136 pages of music (with further sketches and notes for the Coda), do permit a fairly deep insight into Bruckner's creative mind. The mood of the opening is nervous and mysterious, fascinatingly ambiguous and astringent in its harmony. Later on a more assertive chorale theme appears which becomes fused with a motif from the Te Deum. This appearance of the opening figuration of the Te Deum is entirely in keeping with Bruckner's habit of quotation from his sacred choral works (as seen in Symphonies 0, 2, 3, 7 and the Adagio of No. 9). It has been quite erroneously assumed, however, that he was at this point writing a transition to lead into the earlier work, thus providing the symphony with a choral finale. Such a view is untenable as the dying composer can only have suggested the substitution of the Te Deum as a finale as a very desperate solution. The unrelated keys of the two works, and the fact that the appearance of the Te Deum motif can be viewed as an entirely characteristic and symbolic programmatic quotation put the idea of appending the Te Deum to this symphony beyond the bounds of likelihood. This unjustifiable coupling of the two works was in fact perpetrated by Ferdinand Löwe at the first performance on 11 February 1903, allegedly in accordance with the wishes of the late composer, and others followed his example. Indeed the very existence of an independent finale was tacitly ignored for about three decades until Alfred Orel's publication of Bruckner's incomplete 'song of praise to our Lord'. Two projected reconstructions have been issued on disc: one by Nicola Samale and Giuseppe Mazzuka[1], the other by William Carragan[2]. The latter recording also includes the existing fragments (as then known) realized for orchestra from Bruckner's own sketches and played by the Oslo Philharmonic Orchestra. An appendix to Volume IX of the Critical Complete Bruckner Edition now contains all recently discovered additional material (edited by John A. Phillips) and is the last possible scientific score of Bruckner's final symphonic statement unless, of course, something more than a first violin part turns up.

During Bruckner's Linz years his friend Moritz von Mayfeld dedicated a poem to him, the first and last lines of which were used as a couplet and inscribed upon the first laurel wreath awarded to the composer:

Art had its beginning in God—
And so it must lead back to God.

[1] Melodram label: CD989/1–2 (1986).
[2] Chandos label: CD8468/9 and cassette tape DBTB 2010 (1986).

This is the simple motto which accompanied Bruckner throughout every stage of his art. It is the credo that gave him the purpose to fight mental and physical strains until the last morning of his life when the flame flickered out upon the movement that stands as a symbolic last statement of one 'whom death could not daunt'.

Appendix A

Calendar

Year	Age	Life	Contemporary musicians and events
1824		Joseph Anton Bruckner born, 4 Sept., at Ansfelden in Upper Austria, son of Anton Bruckner senior (1791–1837), schoolmaster and village organist, and his wife Theresia, *née* Helm (1801–60), eldest of eleven children, five of whom survived infancy.	Cornelius born, 24 Dec.; Reinecke born, 23 June; Smetana born, 2 March. Abt aged 5; Adam 21; Alkan 11; Assmayer 34; Auber 42; Beethoven 54: Missa Solemnis 1st perf., St Petersburg, and Ninth Symphony, Vienna; Bellini 23; Sterndale Bennett 8; Berlioz 20; Berwald 28; Cherubini 64; Chopin 14; Czerny 33; Dargomizhsky 11; Donizetti 27; Field 42; Franck 2; Franz 9; Glinka 20; Gossec 90; Gounod 6; Halévy 25; Hummel 46; Kalkbrenner 39; Kuhlau 38; Lalo 1; Liszt 13; Loewe 28; Lortzing 22; Marschner 29; Mendelssohn 15; Meyerbeer 33; Offenbach 5; Paganini 42; Raff 2; Reicha 54; Rossini 32; Salieri 74; Schubert 27; Schumann 14; Sechter 36; Spohr 40; Spontini 50; Johann Strauss (I) 20; Verdi 11; Vieuxtemps 4; Wagner 11; Weber 38; Zelter 66
1825	1		Hanslick born, 11 Sept.; Salieri (75) dies, 7 May; Johann Strauss (II) born, 25 Oct. Beethoven (55): String Quartet Op. 132; Schubert (28): 'Great' C major Symphony.

Year	Age	Life	Contemporary musicians and events
1826	2		Weber (39) dies, 4–5 June. Mendelssohn (17): Music for *A Midsummer Night's Dream*.
1827	3		Beethoven (56) dies, 26 Mar. Heine (30): *Buch der Lieder*.
1828	4		Schubert (31) dies, 19 Nov. (last works include String Quintet in C, last 3 Piano Sonatas).
1929	5	Shows keen interest in music and is encouraged in playing violin and spinet by his father, who gives him his first lessons. Birth of sister Rosalia, 17 Feb.	Gossec (95) dies, 16 Feb.; Anton Rubinstein born, 28 Nov. Rossini (37): *Guillaume Tell*.
1830	6	Birth of sister Josefa, 13 Mar.	Bülow born, 8 Jan. Franz Klenze (46) designs the Walhalla near Regensburg. Berlioz (26): *Symphonie Fantastique*.
1831	7		Joachim born, 28 June. Bellini (30): *La Sonnambula, Norma*.
1832	8		Clementi (80) dies, 10 Mar.; Kuhlau (45) dies, 12 Mar.; Goethe (82) dies, 22 Mar.: *Faust* Part 2 published. Zelter (74) dies, 15 May; First railway in mainland Europe, Budweis–Linz, opened.
1833	9	J. B. Weiss (1813–50) acts as godfather at Bruckner's confirmation, 1 June. Birth of brother Ignaz, 28 July.	Borodin born, 12 Nov.; Brahms born, 7 May. Mendelssohn (24): 'Italian' Symphony.
1834	10	Already deputizing for his father at the church organ.	Reubke born, 23 Mar. Berlioz (30): *Harold in Italy*.
1835	11	Moves in the spring to Hörsching, near Linz, and his education continues under Weiss. Hears sacred music of Haydn and Mozart. First compositions: organ and choral pieces.	Bellini (33) dies, 24 Sept.; Cui born, 18 Jan.; Draeseke born, 7 Oct.; Saint-Saëns born, 9 Oct. Franz I of Austria dies, succeeded by Ferdinand I. Donizetti (38): *Lucia di Lammermoor*.
1836	12	Birth of sister Maria Anna ('Nani'), 27 June. In December, returns to Ansfelden and performs some of the duties of his father, who is seriously ill.	Delibes born, 21 Feb.; Reicha (66) dies, 28 May. Mendelssohn (25): *St Paul*; Meyerbeer (45): *Les Huguenots*.

Year	Age	Life	Contemporary musicians and events
1837	13	Father dies, 7 June. Accepted as a choirboy at *Stift* St Florian although his voice is nearly broken. General education continues with organ lessons from Kattinger, violin lessons from Gruber and figured-bass lessons from Bogner. A number of small choral and organ works already composed.	Balakirev born, 12 Jan.; Field (54) dies, 11 Jan.; Hummel (58) dies, 17 Oct. Berlioz (33): *Grande messe des morts*. Lortzing (36): *Zar und Zimmermann*.
1838	14		Bizet born, 25 Oct.; Bruch born, 6 Jan.
1839	15		Mussorgsky born, 21 Mar. Rheinberger born, 17 Mar. Mendelssohn (30) conducts posthumous première of Schubert's 'Great' C major Symphony.
1840	16	Decides on a teaching career, passes entrance examination for the teacher-training college in Linz, 1 Oct., and begins the 10-month course. Studies under J. N. A. Dürrnberger (40). Hears symphonies by Mozart and Beethoven.	Paganini (57) dies, 27 May; Tchaikovsky born, 7 May. Schumann (30): *Frauenliebe und -leben*.
1841	17	Passes final exam in Linz, 30 July, and becomes a qualified assistant teacher. In October is appointed to a school at Windhaag, near Freystadt (Upper Austria).	Chabrier born, 18 Jan.; Dvořák born, 8 Sept.; Schumann (31): 'Spring' Symphony.
1842	18	Suffers much hardship in Windhaag, having to perform menial duties. Plays second fiddle in a band at village entertainments. Composes a small Mass in C.	Cherubini (81) dies, 15 Mar.; Massenet born, 12 May; Sullivan born, 13 May. Philharmonic Society of New York founded. Mendelssohn (33): 'Scottish' Symphony.
1843	19	Transferred to Kronstorf, a smaller village between Enns and Steyr, 23 Jan. A happier time ensues, and musical studies continue under Leopold von Zenetti of Enns (38), including further study of Bach.	Grieg born, 15 June.
1844	20	Composes a Mass for Maundy Thursday.	Verdi (31): *Ernani*.

Year	Age	Life	Contemporary musicians and events
1845	21	Passes his second teaching examination, 29 May, with great success. Growing reputation as an improviser at the organ. Appointed assistant teacher at St Florian, 25 Sept.	Fauré born, 12 May; Widor born, 24 Feb. Wagner (32): *Tannhäuser*.
1846	22	Composition of small choral works continues.	Berlioz (42): *La damnation de Faust*; Mendelssohn (37): *Elijah*; Schumann (36): Symphony No. 2. Pope Pius IX (54) elected.
1847	23	Greatly impressed on hearing Mendelssohn's *St Paul* in Linz.	Mendelssohn (38) dies, 4 Nov.
1848	24	Enrols temporarily in the National Guard as a result of the 1848 revolutions. Appointed provisional organist at St Florian.	Donizetti (50) dies, 8 Apr.; Duparc born, 21 Jan.; Parry born, 27 Feb. Serfdom abolished in Austria. Ferdinand I abdicates in favour of Franz Josef I.
1849	25	Completes his first notable work, Requiem in D minor, first performed at St Florian, 13 Mar.	Chopin (39) dies, 17 Oct.; Kalkbrenner (63) dies, 10 June; Johann Strauss I (45) dies, 25 Sept.
1850	26	Studies Latin, and begins two-year course to improve his educational qualifications. Suicide of J. B. Weiss (37).	Joseph Paxton designs Crystal Palace, London (–1851). Schumann (40): 'Rhenish' Symphony.
1851	27	Works as a voluntary clerk in a local court of law. Attraction to Aloisia Bogner (16), unreciprocated like so many more infatuations with much younger girls.	d'Indy born, 27 Mar.; Spontini (76) dies, 14 Jan.; Lortzing (49) dies, 21 Jan.
1852	28	Visits the court composer Assmayer (61) in Vienna. Composes Magnificat, Psalm 114 and Psalm 22.	Stanford born, 30 Sept.
1853	29		Liszt (42): Sonata in B minor.
1854	30	Composes Missa Solemnis in B flat minor, first performed St Florian, 14 Sept., with great success. Passes an organ examination, 9 Oct., with Assmayer, Sechter, and Preyer as examiners.	Humperdinck born, 1 Sept.; Janáček born, 3 July. Hanslick (29): *Vom Musikalisch-Schönen*. Pius IX declares dogma of the Immaculate Conception of the Blessed Virgin Mary to be an article of faith. The New Cathedral in Linz planned (completed 1924).

Year	Age	Life	Contemporary musicians and events
1855	31	Passes examination in Linz, 25–6 Jan., qualifying him as a high-school teacher. Robert Führer (48) visits St Florian, April, and gives him a splendid testimonial. Bruckner visits Sechter (67) in Vienna and becomes his pupil, July. The Linz Cathedral organist, Wenzel Pranghofer, dies, and Bruckner distinguishes himself at the preliminary examination of candidates, 13 Nov.	Liadov born, 11 May.
1856	32	Appointed organist at Linz Cathedral, at final audition, 25 Jan. Becomes involved in many musical activities; receives tuition by post from Sechter and for the next 5 years often spends Lent and Advent with him. Virtually gives up composition for this period.	Adam (52) dies, 3 May; Schumann (46) dies, 29 July. Wagner (43) completes *Die Walküre*.
1857	33		Czerny (66) dies, 15 July; Elgar born, 2 June; Glinka (52) dies, 15 Feb.
1858	34	Passes exam in harmony, figured bass and organ playing, 10 July.	Leoncavallo born, 8 Mar.; Puccini born, 22 June; Hans Rott born, 1 Aug.; Reubke (24) dies, 3 June. The Ringstrasse, Vienna, begun. Franck (36): *Messe Solonnelle*.
1859	35	Passes elementary counterpoint, 12 Aug.	Sophr (75) dies, 22 Oct. Wagner (46) completes *Tristan*. Liszt (48): *Faust Symphony*.
1860	36	Passes advanced counterpoint, 3 Apr. Bruckner's mother dies, 11 Nov. Appointed conductor of the *Liedertafel 'Frohsinn'*, Nov.	Albéniz born, 29 May; Mahler born, 7 July; Paderewski born, 6 Nov.; Rezniček born, 4 May; Wolf born, 13 Mar.
1861	37	Passes canon and fugue, 26 Mar., concluding his studies with Sechter. Composes a fine 7-part Ave Maria, 12 May. Resigns from *Liedertafel*. Sept. Commences studies of form	Arensky born, 11 Aug.; Marschner (66) dies, 14 Dec. Outbreak of American Civil War.

Year	Age	Life	Contemporary musicians and events
1861		and orchestration with Otto Kitzler (27). Passes an organ exam at the Piaristenkirche, Vienna, and concludes with a magnificent improvisation, Nov. 22. Psalm 146 and 'Afferentur regi' first performed at St Florian, Dec. 14.	
1862	38	Composes String Quartet; 4 pieces for Orchestra. Is introduced to the music of Wagner (49).	Debussy born, 22 Aug. Delius born, 29 Jan.; Halévy (62) dies, 17 Mar.; Assmayer (72) dies, 31 Aug.
1863	39	Composes Overture in G minor, Symphony in F minor and *Germanenzug*. Attends 1st Linz perf. of *Tannhäuser*. Finishes studies with Kitzler and meets Ignaz Dorn (33?) who introduces him to scores of Berlioz and Liszt. Meets Lachner (60) in Munich, Sept.	Josef Wöss born, 13 June; Mascagni born, 7 Dec.
1864	40	Composes Mass in D minor, completed 29 Sept. and first performed at Linz, 20 Nov.	d'Albert born, 10 Apr.; Grechaninov born 25 Oct.; Meyerbeer (72) dies, 2 May; Richard Strauss born, 11 June. Archduke Maximilian of Austria (32) becomes Emperor of Mexico.
1865	41	Begins Symphony No. 1, Jan. Meets Wagner (52), Bülow (35) and Rubinstein (36) and hears *Tristan und Isolde* in Munich, June. Meets Liszt (54) in Pest.	Dukas born, 1 Oct.; Glazunov born, 10 Aug.; Nielsen born, 2 Oct.; Sibelius born, 8 Dec. Liszt (54): *Missa Choralis*.
1866	42	His sister 'Nani' joins him in Linz. Hears Beethoven's Ninth for first time. Completes Symphony No. 1, and on 25 Nov. completes his Mass in E minor. Meets Berlioz (62). At end of year suffers severe depression and a total nervous collapse.	Busoni born, 1 Apr.: Satie born, 17 Mar. Liszt (55): *Christus*.
1867	43	Enters a sanatorium for three months, 8 May to 8 Aug. Applies to *Hofkapelle* and Vienna University for positions, unsuccessfully. Begins Mass in	Granados born, 29 July; Koechlin born, 27 Nov.; Sechter (79) dies, 10 Sept. Wagner (55) completes *Die Meistersinger*, Oct. Emperor

Year	Age	Life	Contemporary musicians and events
1867		F minor (for which he has already made sketches), 14 Sept.	Maximilian (36) executed in Mexico, 19 June. J. Strauss II (42): Waltz, *The Blue Danube*.
1868	44	Re-appointed conductor of Linz *Liedertafel*. Composes motets, including 'Pange lingua' and 'Inveni David'. Conducts the first performance of the finale to Wagner's *Die Meistersinger* in Linz, 4 Apr. and first performance of Symphony No. 1 in Linz, 9 May. Is persuaded by Herbeck (37) to accept a professorship at the Vienna Conservatory in succession to Sechter. Moves to Vienna. Completes Mass in F minor, 9 Sept. Begins teaching in Vienna, 1 Oct.	Bantock born, 7 Aug.; Schillings born, 19 Apr.; Berwald (71) dies, 3 Apr.; Rossini (76) dies, 15 Nov. Grieg (25): Piano Concerto.
1869	45	Composes Symphony No. 0, 24 Jan. to 12 Sept. Visits France, giving distinguished recitals at Nancy and Notre Dame, Paris, April–May. Mass in E minor first performed, Linz, 29 Sept. Composes 'Locus iste'. Vienna Philharmonic reject Symphony No. 1.	Berlioz (65) dies, 8 Mar.; Dargomizhsky (55) dies, 17 Jan.; Loewe (72) dies, 20 Apr.; Pfitzner born, 5 May; Roussel born, 5 Apr.
1870	46	His sister 'Nani' dies, 16 Jan. Appointed teacher at St Anna teacher-training college.	Lehár born, Apr. 30. Dogma of Papal Infallibility in matters of faith and morals declared by Vatican Council, 18 July.
1871	47	Visits London to give recitals at the Albert Hall and Crystal Palace and is praised for his improvisations, Aug. Returns to Vienna to face a disciplinary action at the College of St Anna. Begins Symphony No. 2 and makes a sketch of 67 bars for a Symphony in B flat major.	Auber (89) dies, 12 May. Royal Albert Hall opened, London. Verdi (58): *Aida*.
1872	48	Conducts first performance of Mass in F minor, 16 June. Completes Symphony No. 2, 11 Sept.; it is rejected by the Vienna Philharmonic.	Scriabin born, 4 Jan.; Vaughan Williams born, 12 Oct.

Year	Age	Life	Contemporary musicians and events
1873	49	Composes Symphony No. 3, completed 31 Dec. Visits Marienbad, Karlsbad, and Bayreuth. Again meets Wagner (60), who accepts dedication of Symphony No. 3. Conducts first performance of Symphony No. 2, Vienna, 26 Oct.	Rakhmaninov born, 1 Apr.; Reger born, 19 Mar.
1874	50	Composes Symphony No. 4, completed 22 Nov. Makes several applications to Vienna University for a lectureship but is opposed by Hanslick (49). Loses his position at the College of St Anna and worries about his financial prospects. His sister Josefa dies, 3 July. Symphony No. 3 revised, and rejected by the Vienna Philharmonic.	Cornelius (49) dies, 26 Oct.; Holst born, 21 Sept.; Ives born, 20 Oct.; Franz Schmidt born, 22 Dec.; Schoenberg born, 13 Sept. Verdi (61): Requiem.
1875	51	Begins Symphony No. 5, 14 Feb. Sketches 18 bars of a Requiem in D minor, Sept. Appointed lecturer in harmony and counterpoint at Vienna University, July.	Sterndale Bennett (58) dies, 1 Feb.; Bizet (37) dies, 3 June; Coleridge-Taylor born, 15 Aug.; Glière born, 11 Jan.; Ravel born, 7 Mar.; Tovey born, 17 July.
1876	52	Conducts performance of Symphony No. 2, Vienna, 20 Feb., and revises it, making some cuts. Completes first draft of Symphony No. 5, 16 May, and commences revising both it and Symphony No. 3. Revises the 3 great Masses. Attends the first 'Ring' cycle at Bayreuth.	Havergal Brian born, 29 Jan.; Falla born, 23 Nov.; Schelling born, 26 July. Dessoff (41) conducts première of Symphony No. 1 by Brahms (43).
1877	53	Moves to a new flat. Completes Symphony No. 5, Aug. Conducts disastrous first performance of Symphony No. 3, 16 Dec., but Rättig publishes it and Mahler (17), with whom Bruckner becomes friendly, helps make a piano reduction of it.	Dohnányi born, 27 July; Karg-Elert born, 21 Nov. Richter (34) conducts première of Symphony No. 2 by Brahms (44). Herbeck (45) dies, 28 Oct.
1878	54	Begins a thorough revision of Symphony No. 4. Further revisions of Symphonies 3 and 5. Appointed full member of	Boughton born, 23 Jan.; Schreker born, 23 Mar. Pius IX (85) dies, 7 Feb.; Leo XIII elected Pope.

Year	Age	Life	Contemporary musicians and events
1878		*Hofkapelle* where he has worked as honorary organist-designate since 1868. Composes 'Tota pulchra es Maria' and begins String Quintet.	
1879	55	Composes 'Os justi' and completes String Quintet, 12 July. Begins Symphony No. 6, 24 Sept. and writes Intermezzo for String Quintet, Dec.	Bridge born, 26 Feb.; Ireland born, 13 Aug.; Respighi born, 9 July; Scott (Cyril) born, 27 Sept. Tchaikovsky (39): *Eugene Onegin.*
1880	56	Completes revision of Symphony No. 4, 5 June, and continues work on Symphony No. 6. A holiday includes a visit to Oberammergau and a tour of Switzerland.	Bloch born, 24 July; Medtner born, 5 Jan.; Offenbach (61) dies, 4 Oct. Mahler (20): *Das klagende Lied.*
1881	57	First performance of Symphony No. 4, 20 Feb. (under Richter, 37). Begins Te Deum, completes Symphony No. 6, 3 Sept., and begins Symphony No. 7, 23 Sept. First performance of Quintet (incomplete), 17 Nov.	Bartók born, 25 Mar.; Miaskovsky born, 20 Apr.; Mussorgsky (42) dies, 28 Mar. Verdi (68): revision of *Simon Boccanegra.*
1882	58	Continues work on Symphony No. 7. Visits Bayreuth to hear first performance of *Parsifal* and sees Wagner (69) for the last time.	Grainger born, 8 July; Kodály born, 16 Dec.; Raff (60) dies, 24–5 June; Stravinsky born, 17 June; Szymanowski born, 6 Oct.
1883	59	Movements 2 and 3 of Symphony No. 6 first performed, 11 Feb. (under Wilhelm Jahn). Visits Wagner's grave at Bayreuth, Aug. Completes Symphony No. 7 at St Florian, 5 Sept. Begins final version of Te Deum, 28 Sept.	Bax born, 6 Nov.; Casella born, 25 July; Wagner (69) dies, 13 Feb.; Webern born, 3 Dec. Brahms (50): Symphony No. 3.
1884	60	Completes Te Deum, 7 Mar. Visits Prague, and later Bayreuth and Munich. Friendship with Hugo Wolf (24). Spends sixtieth birthday quietly in Vöcklabruck. Begins Symphony No. 8. Symphony No. 7 first performed in Leipzig, 30 Dec. (under Nikisch, 29) and is a tremendous success.	Smetana (60) dies, 12 May; Hans Rott (25) dies, 25 June. Debussy (22): *L'Enfant prodigue.*

Year	Age	Life	Contemporary musicians and events
1885	61	Composes 'Ecce sacerdos' and 'Virga Jesse'. Continues to work on Symphony No. 8 (until 1887). First New York performances of Symphonies Nos. 3 and 7.	Abt (65) dies, 31 Mar.; Berg born, 9 Feb.; Butterworth born, 12 July; Varèse born, 22 Dec.; Wellesz born, 21 Oct. Brahms (52): Symphony No. 4.
1886	62	First performance of Te Deum with orchestra, Vienna, 10 Jan. (under Richter, 42). First Vienna performance of Symphony No. 7, March (Richter). Awarded Order of Franz-Josef by the Emperor. Visits Bayreuth, and plays at the funeral of Liszt, 3 Aug.	Liszt (74) dies, 31 July. Saint-Säens (51): *Organ Symphony*. Robert Haas born, 15 Aug.
1887	63	Created honorary member of the Dutch *Maatschappij tot Bevordering der Toonkunst*. First London performance of Symphony No. 7, 23 May. Completes Symphony No. 8 but the failure by Levi (48) to understand it causes a severe deterioration in his nervous condition and a period of 'revision mania' begins with work on Symphony No. 8. Commences Symphony No. 9.	Borodin (53) dies, 28 Feb.; Villa-Lobos born, 5 Mar. Goldmark (47): *Rustic Wedding* Symphony.
1888	64	First 'all Bruckner' concert in Vienna, Jan. (under Richter, 44). Revision of Symphony No. 3 commenced with J. Schalk (31).	Alkan (74) dies, 29 Mar. Mahler (28): Symphony No. 1. Satie (22): *Gymnopédies*.
1889	65	Created an honorary member of the *Richard Wagner-Verein*. Spends a social evening with Brahms (56). Completes new version of Symphony No. 3 and continues revising Symphony No. 8.	R. Strauss (25): *Don Juan*. Tchaikovsky (49): Symphony No. 5. Adolf Hitler born, 30 April.
1890	66	Created honorary member of the Austrian Diet, with a stipend. Chronic catarrh of the larynx aggravates his health which is now hampered by dropsy. Relinquishes duties as organ professor at the	Franck (67) dies, 8 Nov.; F. Martin born, 15 Sept.; Martinů born, 8 Dec. Elgar (33): Overture *Froissart*. Wolf (30): *Spanisches Liederbuch*.

Year	Age	Life	Contemporary musicians and events
1890		Conservatory. Publications continue during the last years. Completes revision of Symphony No. 8, 10 Mar., and begins a new version of Symphony No. 1, 12 Mar. Plays at the wedding of the emperor's daughter, Marie Valerie, in Ischl, 31 July. Final revision of Third Symphony premièred by Richter (47), 21 Dec.	
1891	67	Completes new version of Symphony No. 1, 18 Apr.; 1st perf., 13 Dec. Attends perf. of Te Deum in Berlin, 31 May (under Ochs, 33). Visits Bayreuth, Aug. Receives honorary doctorate of Vienna University, 7 Nov. Continues work on Symphony No. 9.	Bliss born, 2 Aug.; Delibes (54) dies, 16 Jan.; Prokofiev born, 23 Apr. Rakhmaninov (18): Piano Concerto No. 1. Wolf (31): *Italienisches Liederbuch*.
1892	68	Composes Psalm 150, first perf. 13 Nov., 'Das deutsche Lied' and 'Vexilla regis'. Symphony No. 8 first perf. 18 Dec. (under Richter, 49).	Franz (77) dies, 24 Oct.; Honegger born, 10 Mar.; Lalo (69) dies, 22 Apr.; Milhaud born, 4 Sept. Nielsen (27): Symphony No. 1.
1893	69	Created honorary member of the *Gesellschaft der Musikfreunde*. Composes *Helgoland*, completed 7 Aug. Confined to bed, seriously ill, for much of the year. Makes his will, 10 Nov., preserving his 'original scores' 'for future times'. Mental condition deteriorates. Scherzo of Symphony No. 9 completed, 27 Feb., and first movement completed 23 Dec.	Gounod (75) dies, 18 Oct.; Hellmesberger (64) dies, 24 Oct.; Tchaikovsky (53) dies, 6 Nov. Dvořák (52): Symphony *From the New World*. Humperdinck (39): *Hänsel und Gretel*.
1894	70	Visits Berlin with Wolf (33) for concerts of their music, Jan., but is too ill to attend first perf. of Symphony No. 5, Graz, 8 Apr. (F. Schalk). Spends seventieth birthday in Steyr and receives many honours.	Bülow (64) dies, 12 Feb.; Chabrier (53) dies, 13 Sept.; Anton Rubinstein (64) dies, 20 Nov. Debussy (32): *Prélude à l'après-midi d'un faune*.

Year	Age	Life	Contemporary musicians and events
1894		Receives the freedom of the city of Linz, 15 Nov. Resigns from the University. Completes the Adagio of Symphony No. 9, 30 Nov. and presses on with the Finale.	
1895	71	Continues work on the Finale of Symphony No. 9 despite weakening mental and physical condition. Moves to a gate-keeper's lodge at the Schloss Belvedere, placed at his disposal by the emperor, July.	Hindemith born, 16 Nov.; Orff born, 10 July. R. Strauss (31): *Till Eulenspiegel.* Sibelius (30): *The Swan of Tuonela.*
1896	72	Attends his last concert, a performance of the Te Deum, 12 Jan. In his last weeks serious depression and a tendency towards religious mania set in. On Sunday 11 Oct., works on the finale of the Symphony in the morning and dies quietly later in the day. Funeral held in the Karlskirche, Vienna, 14 Oct. and his body is laid to rest in St Florian.	Gerhard born, 25 Sept. Albéniz aged 36; Arensky 35; Balakirev 59; Bantock 28; Bartók 15; Bax 12; Berg 11; Bliss 5; Bloch 16; Boughton 18; Brahms 63; Havergal Brian 20; Bridge 17; Bruch 58; Busoni 30; Butterworth 11; Casella 13; Coleridge-Taylor 21; Cui 61; d'Albert 32; Debussy 34; Delius 34; Dohnányi 19; Draeseke 61; Dukas 31; Duparc 48; Dvořák 55: (Symphonic Poems Opp. 107–10); Elgar 39: *King Olaf*; Falla 19; Fauré 51; Glazunov 31; Glière 21; Grainger 14; Granados 29; Grechaninov 31; Grieg 53; Hanslick 71; Hindemith 1; Holst 22; Honegger 4; Humperdinck 42; d'Indy 45; Ireland 17; Ives 21; Janáček 42; Joachim 65; Karg-Elert 18; Kodály 13; Koechlin 28; Leoncavallo 38; Liadov 41; Mahler 36: completes Symphony No. 3; F. Martin 6; Martinů 5; Mascagni 32; Massenet 54; Medtner 16; Miaskovsky 15; Milhaud 4; Nielsen 31; Orff 1; Paderewski 36; Parry 48;

Bruckner

Year   Age   Life
1896

Contemporary musicians and events
Pfitzner 27; Prokofiev 5;
Puccini 38: *La Bohème*;
Rakhmaninov 23; Ravel 21;
Reger 23; Respighi 17;
Reznicek 36; Rheinberger 57;
Rimsky-Korsakov 52;
Roussel 27; Saint-Säens 61;
Satie 30; Schelling 20;
Schillings 28; Schmidt 21;
Schoenberg 22; Schreker 18;
Scott (Cyril) 17; Sibelius 30;
Skryabin 24; Stanford 44;
J. Strauss (II) 70; R. Strauss
32: *Also sprach Zarathustra*;
Stravinsky 14; Sullivan 54;
Szymanowski 14; Tovey 21;
Varèse 10; Vaughan Williams
24; Verdi 83; Villa-Lobos 9;
Webern 12; Wellesz 10;
Widor 52; Wolf 36: *Der
Corregidor*; Wöss, 33.

Appendix B

List of works

(1) BRGA = *Anton Bruckner: Kritische Gesamtausgabe* (1951–), Musikwissenschaftlicher Verlag, Vienna (Anton Bruckner: Critical Complete Edition). The volumes and parts of this edition are given in Roman and Arabic numerals, for example BRGAviii/2 indicates that the work is to be found in part two of volume eight of the complete edition.

(2) An asterisk beside a work or volume from BRGA indicates that a separate volume of critical notes (*Revisionsbericht*), often including important music, is published in the complete edition.[1]

(3) Dates of commencement and completion of many works, individual movements, and sketches can be found in the critical apparatus (*Revisionsberichte*) of BRGA; in F. Blume's catalogue in *Musik in Geschichte und Gegenwart*, volume 2; and in Göllerich and Auer, *Anton Bruckner*, 4 volumes in 9, Regensburg 1922–36, reprinted 1974. The Göllerich–Auer volumes also contain most of the smaller vocal works, piano and organ pieces, and many facsimiles.

LARGE-SCALE SACRED WORKS

Requiem in D minor, WAB 39 (1848–9), SATB soli and chorus, orchestra, and organ (small revisions made in 1854 and 1894); ed. Leopold Nowak 1966, BRGAxiv, and in vocal score ed. Hans Jancik, 1974

Magnificat, WAB 24 (1852), SATB soli and chorus, orchestra, and organ; BRGAxx/3 (in preparation)

Psalm 114, WAB 36, SAATB chorus + 3 trombones (1852); BRGAxx/1 (in preparation)

Psalm 22, WAB 34 (1852), SATB chorus and piano; BRGAxx/2 (in preparation)

Missa Solemnis in B flat minor, WAB 29 (1854), SATB soli and chorus + orchestra; ed. Nowak, 1975, BRGAxv* and in vocal score ed. Jancik, 1977

Psalm 146, WAB 37 (1860), SATB soli, chorus, and orchestra; pub. 1971; BRGAxx/4 (in preparation)

Psalm 112, WAB 35 (1863), double chorus + orchestra, pub. 1926, ed. Wöss; BRGAxx/5 (in preparation)

Mass in D minor, WAB 26 (1864; rev. 1876 and 1881), first pub. 1892; ed. Nowak, 1975, BRGAxvi and in vocal score, ed. F. Löwe, rev. W. Gabriel, 1994

---

[1] For more detailed information contact: Musikwissenschaftlicher Verlag, A–1010 Wien, Dorotheergasse 10, Vienna.

Mass in E minor, WAB 27 (1866: rev. 1869, 1876, and 1882), 8-part chorus and wind instruments; first pub. 1892; 1866 version ed. Nowak, 1977, BRGAxvii/1; 1882 version ed. Haas and Nowak, 1940; ed. Nowak, 1959, BRGAxvii/2 and in vocal score, ed. C. Hynais, rev. K. Urbanek, 1985

Mass in F minor, WAB 28 (1867–8; rev. 1872, 1876, 1877, 1881, 1883, and 1890–3), SATB soli, chorus, orchestra + organ; first pub. 1894; revision of 1881 pub. 1944 ed. Haas, and 1960 ed. Nowak, BRGAxviii (with revisions based on newly discovered MSS) and in vocal score ed. J. Schalk, rev. Jancik, 1977

Te Deum in C major, WAB 45 (first draft 1881; final version 1883–4), SATB soli, chorus, orchestra + organ; first pub. 1885; ed. Nowak, 1962, BRGAxix and in vocal score ed. J. Schalk, rev. Jancik, 1962

Psalm 150, WAB 38 (1892), soprano solo, chorus + orchestra; pub. 1892; ed. F. Grasberger, 1964, BRGAxx/6 and in vocal score ed. C. Hynais, rev. W. Gabriel, 1987

SMALLER SACRED WORKS

(1) All works listed in this section are for 4-part mixed chorus (SATB) unless stated otherwise.

(2) All works listed in this section can be found in BRGAxxi*.

Pange lingua, C major, a cappella, WAB 31 (1835 or 1836; rev. 1891)

Mass in C major, for contralto solo, two horns, and organ, WAB 25 (1842)

Libera, F major, with organ, WAB 21 (*c.* 1843)

Asperges me, F major, a cappella *or* with organ, WAB 4 (1843 or 1844)

Mass for Maundy Thursday, F major, a cappella, WAB 146 (1844) ('Choral Messe ohne Kyrie und Gloria für den Gründonnerstag')

2 *Asperges me*, with organ, WAB 3 (by 1845)

Tantum ergo (*Pange lingua*), D major, a cappella, WAB 32 (1845?)

Tantum ergo, A major, with organ, WAB 43 (1845?)

Chorale: 'Dir, Herr, Dir will ich mich ergeben', a cappella, WAB 12 (1844 or 1845)

Herz Jesu Lied: 'Aus allen Herzen eines', with organ (*c.* 1846)

4 *Tantum ergo*, B flat, A flat, E flat, C major; with organ ad libitum, WAB 41 (1846; rev. 1888)

Tantum ergo, D major, for 5-part chorus (SSATB) and organ, WAB 42 (February 1846; rev. 1888)

Passion Chorale: 'In jener letzten der Nächte', a cappella, WAB 17 (with a version for voice and piano) (*c.* 1848)

Zwei Totenlieder, E flat major, F major; a cappella, WAB 47–8 (1852)

Libera, F minor, for 5-part chorus (SSATB), three trombones, cello, double bass, and organ, WAB 22 (1854)

Tantum ergo, B flat major, with two trumpets, strings, and organ, WAB 44 (*c.* 1854)

O du liebes Jesu Kind, solo voice and organ (?1855)

Ave Maria, F major, with cello and organ, WAB 5 (24 July 1856)

Ave Maria, for 7-part chorus (SAATTBB) a cappella, WAB 6 (1861)

Afferentur regi, with three trombones and organ ad libitum, WAB 1 (13 December 1861)

Pange lingua et Tantum ergo (Phrygian), a cappella, WAB 33 (31 January 1868)
Inveni David, for 4-part male chorus and 4 trombones, WAB 19 (21 April 1868)
Iam lucis orto sidere (*In St Angelum custodem*), a cappella and a version with
  organ, WAB 18 (1868; rev. 1886 for 4-part male chorus a cappella)
Locus iste, a cappella, WAB 23 (11 August 1869)
Christus factus est, for 8-part chorus (SSAATTBB), three trombones, and strings
  ad libitum, WAB 10 (1873; rev. later)
Tota pulchra es Maria, with tenor solo and organ, WAB 46 (30 March 1878)
Os justi, a cappella, WAB 30 (July 1879)
Ave Maria, F major, solo contralto with piano, organ or harmonium, WAB 7 (5
  February 1882)
Veni Creator Spiritus, harmonized plainsong, WAB 50 (1884 or earlier)
Christus factus est, D minor, a cappella, WAB 11 (28 may 1884)
Salvum fac populum tuum, a cappella, WAB 40 (14 November 1884)
Ecce sacerdos magnus, with three trombones and organ, WAB 13 (April 1885)
Virga Jesse floruit, a cappella, WAB 52 (3 September 1885)
Ave Regina coelorum, harmonized plainsong, WAB 8 (*c.* 1885–8)
Vexilla Regis, a cappella, WAB 51 (9 February 1892)

ORCHESTRAL WORKS

March in D minor, WAB 96 (1862). First pub. 1934 with the following item as '4
  Orchestral Pieces', ed. Orel
3 Orchestral Pieces (E flat major, E minor, F major), WAB 97 (1862), ed. Hans
  Jancik and Rüdiger Bornhöft (with the March in D minor), BRGAxii/4* (in
  preparation)
Apollo-Marsch for military band, WAB 115 (1862?)
Overture in G minor, WAB 98 (1862–3). Pub. 1921; and 1934 ed. Orel; ed. Jancik
  and Bornhöft, BRGAxii/5 (in preparation)
Symphony in F minor, WAB 99 (1863)
  Andante pub., 1913, ed. Hynais.
  Full piano version pub. in Göllerich–Auer III/2, 1930.
  Full score pub. 1973, ed. Nowak, BRGAx*
March in E flat major for military band, WAB 116 (1865) ed. Bornhöft.
  BRGAxii/8* (in preparation)
Symphony No. 1 in C minor, WAB 101
  'Linz Version' (1865–6). First pub. 1935, ed. Haas; ed. Nowak, 1953, BRGAi/1
  Original (rejected) Scherzo and fragment of the original Adagio, ed. Wolfgang
  Grandjean, 1995, BRGAi/1*
  'Vienna Version', 1890–1. First pub. 1893, ed. Hynais; ed. Haas, 1935; ed.
  Günter Brosche, 1980, BRGAi/2
Symphony No. 0 in D minor, WAB 100 (1869—perhaps based on earlier sketches)
  First pub. 1924, ed. Wöss.
  Definitive original score ed. Nowak, 1968, BRGAxi*
Symphony No. 2 in C minor, WAB 102 (1871–2)
  First pub. ed. Haas, 1938.
  Definitive original score (1872), ed. William Carragan, BRGAii/1 (in prepara-
  tion)
  Rev. 1876–7, ed. Nowak, 1965, BRGAii/2

Bruckner

Rev. 1891–2, pub. 1892
Symphony No. 3 in D minor, WAB 103 (1872–3)
First pub. ed. Nowak, 1977, BRGAiii/1
Rev. of Adagio, 1876, ed. Nowak, 1980, BRGAiii/1
Rev. of whole symphony, 1877; first pub. 1878; ed. Oeser, 1950; ed. Nowak, 1981, BRGAiii/2
Another complete revision, 1888–9, pub. 1890, ed. F. Schalk; ed. Nowak, 1959, BRGAiii/3
Symphony No. 4 in E flat major, 'Romantic', WAB 104 (1874)
First pub. ed. Nowak, 1975, BRGAiv/1
1878 version of Finale, ed. Nowak, 1981, BRGAiv/2
Rev. of whole symphony (with new 'Hunt' Scherzo, and Finale of 1880), 1878–80 first pub. (with the Finale of 1878 in an appendix) ed. Haas, 1936 and 1944 (with minor revisions); ed. Nowak, 1953, BRGAiv/2 (the Nowak edition incorporates further revisions of 1886).
Rev. by F. Löwe and J. Schalk, 1888–9, pub. 1889
Symphony No. 5 in B flat major, WAB 105 (1875–6); slight revisions 1876–8 and later. First pub. 1896, ed. F. Schalk; ed. Haas, 1935; ed. Nowak, 1951, BRGAv
Symphony No. 6 in A major, WAB 106 (1879–81)
First pub. 1899, ed. Hynais; ed. Haas, 1935; ed. Nowak, 1952, BRGAvi*
Symphony No. 7 in E major, WAB 107 (1881–3)
First pub. 1885 ed. J. Schalk and Löwe; ed. Haas, 1944; ed. Nowak, 1954, BRGAvii
Symphony No. 8 in C minor, WAB 108 (1884–7)
Rev. 1887–90. Revised version first pub. ed. J. Schalk, 1892
ed., Haas, 1939 (the 1890 version with many restorations from the 1887 version).
1887 version ed. Nowak, 1972, BRGAviii/1
1890 version ed. Nowak, 1955, BRGAviii/2
Symphony No. 9 in D minor, WAB 109 (movements 1–3, 1887–94; Finale, unfinished, 1894–6)
First pub. 1903, ed. Löwe; ed. Orel (with sketches for the Finale), 1934; ed. Nowak, 1951, BRGAix; ed. Schönzeler, 1963
Reconstruction of the autograph fragments of the Finale, ed. John A. Phillips, 1994, BRGAix
Reconstruction of 2 rejected Trios, ed. Carragan, as *2 Intermezzi*, New York, 1980

CHAMBER MUSIC

Zwei Aequale for three trombones (alto, tenor, and bass) WAB 114, 149 (January 1847) BRGAxxi
String Quartet in C minor, WAB 111 (1862) pub. 1955, ed. Nowak, BRGAxiii/1*
Rondo for String Quartet in C minor (1862) pub. 1985, ed. Nowak, BRGAxii/1
Abendklänge for violin and piano, WAB 110 (1866) BRGAxii/7
String Quintet in F major (2vns, 2 vas, vc.) WAB 112 (1878–9) first pub. 1884; and ed. Nowak 1963, BRGAxiii/2
Intermezzo in D minor for String Quintet, WAB 113 (1879) first pub. 1913; ed. Nowak, 1963, BRGAxiii/2

ORGAN MUSIC

All works listed in this section will be found in BRGAxii/6 (an edition of all the organ works was issued by Doblinger, Vienna, 1970).

Four Preludes, WAB 128 (*c.* 1836)
Prelude in E flat major, WAB 127 (*c.* 1837)
Two Pieces (Prelude and Postlude), WAB 130, 126 (*c.* 1846/1852)
Prelude and Fugue in C minor, WAB 131 (1847)
Fugue in D minor, WAB 125 (1861)
Prelude in C major, WAB 129 (1884)

SOLO PIANO MUSIC

All works listed in this section can be found in BRGAxii/2*.

Lancier-Quadrille aus beliebten Opernmelodien zusammengestellt, WAB 120 (*c.* 1850)
Steiermärker, WAB 122 (*c.* 1850)
Klavierstück in E flat major, WAB 119 (*c.* 1856)
Sonata movement in G minor (1862); sketch
Stille Betrachtung an einem Herbstabend, WAB 123 (1863)
Erinnerung, WAB 117 (*c.* 1868)
Fantasie in G major, WAB 118 (1868)

PIANO MUSIC FOR 4 HANDS

Three short pieces [for children], WAB 124 (1853–5) BRGAxii/3*
Quadrille, WAB 121 (*c.* 1854) BRGAxii/3*

SONGS

All works in this section will be found in BRGAxxiii/1.

'Frühlingslied' (Heine), WAB 68 (1851)
'Amaranths Waldeslieder' (O. Redwitz), WAB 58 (*c.* 1858)
'Volkslied', WAB 94 (*c.* 1861); also arr. for male-voice chorus
'Im April' (Emanuel Geibel), WAB 75 (1868)
'Mein Herz und deine Stimme' (Platen), WAB 79 (1868)
'Herbstkummer' (Ernst) WAB 72 (*c.* 1868)

WORKS FOR MIXED CHORUS

Cantata, *Vergissmeinnicht* (Marinelli), for solo quartet, 8-part chorus, and piano, WAB 93 (1845), BRGAxxii/1 (3 versions)
Cantata, *Entsagen* (from O. Redwitz's 'Amaranth'), with solo voices, chorus, and organ or piano, WAB 14 (*c.* 1851) BRGAxxii/1
Zwei Totenlieder, WAB 47–8 (1852), BRGAxxi
Cantata, *Auf, Brüder! auf zur frohen Feier* (Marinelli), for male-voice quartet, 6-part chorus, and brass, WAB 61 (1852) BRGAxxii/1
Festive song, *St Jodok, Spross aus edlem Stamm*, with solo voices and piano, WAB 15 (1855) BRGAxxii/1

Bruckner

Cantata, *Auf Brüder, auf, und die Saiten zur Hand* (Marinelli), for male-voice
   quartet, male-voice chorus, 8-part mixed chorus, woodwind, and brass,
   WAB 60 (1855) BRGAxxii/1
Das edle Herz (Marinelli), WAB 66 (1861) (2nd setting; see also Works for Male-
   Voice Chorus)
Du bist wie eine Blume (Heine), for solo quartet, WAB 64 (1861)
Wahlspruch für den gemischten Chor der Liedertafel Frohsinn in Linz, WAB 95
   (1868)

WORKS FOR MALE-VOICE CHORUS

(1) Unless otherwise stated, works in this section will be found in BRGAxxiii/2.
(2) Unless otherwise stated, all works are TTBB a cappella.

An dem Feste (Alois Knauer), WAB 59 (1843; later twice revised)
Das Lied vom deutschen Vaterland, WAB 78 (*c.* 1845)
Ständchen, WAB 84 (*c.* 1846)
Festlied, WAB 67 (*c.* 1846) from *An dem Feste*, with new text
Der Lehrerstand, WAB 77 (*c.* 1847)
Sternschnuppen (Marinelli), WAB 85 (*c.* 1848)
Zwei Sängersprüche, WAB 83 (1851)
Das edle Herz (Marinelli), WAB 65 (*c.* 1851)
Die Geburt, WAB 69 (1851)
Vor Arneths Grab, WAB 53 (1854) with three trombones
Lasst Jubelklänge laut erklingen (A. Weiss), WAB 76 (1854) with brass instru-
   ments
Des Dankes Wort sei mir gegönnt, WAB 62 (1855) for T and B soli + 5-part male
   chorus
Am Grabe (*Grabgesang*), WAB 2 (1861)
Festive Cantata, *Preiset den Herrn* (Pannesberger), WAB 16 (1862) with baritone
   solo, woodwind, brass + timpani, BRGAxxii/2
Der Abendhimmel I in A flat major (Zedlitz), WAB 55 (1862)
Germanenzug (Silberstein), WAB 70 (1863; first pub. 1865) with brass instru-
   ments, BRGAxxii/2
Herbstlied (F. Sallet), WAB 73 (1864) with 2 sopranos + piano
Um Mitternacht I (R. Prutz), WAB 89 (1864) with contralto solo + piano
Trauungslied (Proschka), WAB 49 (1865) with organ
Der Abendhimmel II in F major (Zedlitz), WAB 56 (1866)
O könnt ich dich beglücken, WAB 92 (1866) with 2 baritones soli
Vaterländisches Weinlied (Silberstein), WAB 91 (1866)
Wahlspruch für die Liedertafel Sierning, WAB 95 (1868)
Motto und Begrüssung, WAB 148 (1869)
Mitternacht (J. Mendelssohn), WAB 80 (1870) with tenor solo + piano
Motto, WAB 148 (1874)
Das hohe Lied (Mattig), WAB 74 (1876) with 3 soloists; 2 versions: (a) a cappella,
   (b) with strings and wind band
Trösterin Musik (A. Seuffert), WAB 88 (1877) with organ
Nachruf (A. Seuffert), WAB 81 (1877) with organ
Zur Vermählungsfeier (Silberstein), WAB 54 (1878)
Abendzauber (Mattig), WAB 57 (1878) with baritone solo, 3 yodellers + 4 horns

142

Sängerbund (Kerschbaum), WAB 82 (1882)
Um Mitternacht II (R. Prutz), WAB 90 (1886) with tenor solo
Träumen und Wachen (Grillparzer), WAB 87 (1890) with tenor solo
Das deutsche Lied (E. Fels), WAB 63 (1892) with brass instruments
Tafellied, WAB 86 (1893) from *An dem Feste*, with new text
Helgoland (Silberstein), WAB 71 (1893) with large orchestra, BRGAxxii/2

UNFINISHED WORKS

Mass without Gloria and Credo, mixed chorus, a cappella (1843–4), BRGAxxi
Missa pro Quadragesima, mixed chorus, organ + three trombones (*c.* 1846),
    BRGAxxi
Mass in E flat major, mixed chorus and orchestra (1845–8), BRGAxxi
Symphony in B flat major (1871); sketch of 67 bars (in Göllerich–Auer iv/1)
Requiem in D minor (1875); beginning only; BRGAxxi

LOST WORKS

Domine ad adjuvandum me, for chorus and instruments (1835)
Litanei, for chorus and wind instruments (1844)
Salve Regina (1844)
Requiem, for male chorus and organ (1845)
Litanei (*c.* 1856)
Zigeunerwaldlied, for male chorus (1863)

Appendix C

Personalia

Adler, Guido (1855–1941). Austrian critic and distinguished musicologist, born in Moravia. A pupil of Bruckner and also of Dessoff at the Vienna Conservatory until 1874 when he entered the University of Vienna and, with Mottl and others, founded its Wagner Society. Reader in musical history at the German University of Prague, 1885–97, and succeeded Hanslick in the chair for music history and aesthetics at the University of Vienna (1898–1927). Founder and chief editor of the *Denkmäler der Tonkunst in Österreich* (1894–1938), 83 volumes in all; many of the later issues were edited by Haas. Among his innumerable important writings were *Gustav Mahler* (1916), and his memoirs, *Wollen und Wirken* (1935).

Assmayer, Ignaz (1790–1862). Austrian composer and organist, pupil of Salieri and Michael Haydn, and a friend of Schubert. He wrote several oratorios, 21 Masses, 2 Requiems as well as *c.* 60 instrumental compositions. Appointed court organist at Vienna in 1825 and succeeded Joseph Eybler as first Imperial Kapellmeister in 1846. He was one of Bruckner's examiners in organ playing in 1854.

Auer, Max (1880–1962). Austrian biographer of Bruckner. He completed the official biography begun by August Göllerich and wrote other studies of the composer.

Chrismann, Franz Xaver (1726–95). Notable Austrian organ builder and lay member of the clergy, born in Carniola. He constructed the great organ at St Florian, completing it in 1774. It was rebuilt by M. Mauracher in 1873–5. A restoration of the original organ was completed in 1951. Chrismann's organ for the church of Schottenfeld, Vienna, was particularly admired by Mozart and Albrechtsberger.

Decsey, Ernest (1870–1941). Austro–German author and music critic; first obtained a doctorate in law at Vienna, then became a composition pupil of Bruckner and Robert Fuchs. He published biographies of Bruckner, Debussy, Johann Strauss, and Wolf. Also wrote novels, plays, and librettos.

Dessoff, Otto (1835–92). German conductor and composer. After conducting in various small towns from 1854 to 1860 he became conductor at the Vienna Opera, a professor at the Vienna Conservatory and chief conductor of the Philharmonic concerts in Vienna. After 1875 he occupied similar positions in Karlsruhe (where he gave the première of Brahms's Symphony No. 1 in 1876) and Frankfurt. His daughter, Margarethe Dessoff, moved to New York in 1923 where she founded the Dessoff Choir. He appreciated Bruckner the organist but failed to understand him as a composer.

Dorn, Ignaz (*c*. 1830–1872). Austrian composer, violinist, and conductor. After a period as violinist in the opera orchestra in Vienna he moved to the Linz theatre in 1863 and soon rose from player to become second Kapellmeister. His musical tastes were ultra-modern, he encouraged Bruckner's early symphonic writing, and helped acquaint him with the scores of Wagner, Berlioz, and Liszt.

Dürrnberger, Johann August (1800–80). Teacher of music at Linz and author of a book on musical theory. From 1841 he taught Bruckner harmony and thorough-bass and played an important part in securing Bruckner's post as organist of Linz Cathedral. Another of his pupils, Johann Evangelist Habert, was a teacher of Busoni, founder of the Austrian Caecilian movement, and admirer of Bruckner's E minor Mass.

Eckstein, Friedrich (1861–1939). Austrian journalist, philosopher, and industrialist; notable musical amateur and a 'character' in Viennese musical circles at the turn of the century. He published valuable memoirs of Bruckner as man and teacher, and supported his works financially.

Führer, Robert (1807–61). Organist and composer, born in Prague. He held posts at Prague, Gmunden, Ischl, Salzburg, Munich, Augsburg, and Vienna. He published 32 Masses, 14 Requiems and much other sacred music. Lost his position in several cities owing to his irregular life, embezzlements, etc., and his doubtful honesty is revealed in an attempt he made to pass off a Mass of Schubert's as his own, having added trumpets and drums to it. Despite his notoriety he always won admiration for his fine playing and musicianship. He encouraged Bruckner to study with Sechter. He sought unsuccessfully to succeed Bruckner as organist at St Florian in 1855.

Haas, Robert (1886–1960). Musicologist, conductor, and composer of songs and chamber music, born in Prague. Librarian of the music department of the Vienna Stadtbibliothek from 1920, professor at Vienna University from 1930; he retired in 1945. Beside Nowak, he was the foremost editor of Bruckner's scores; also a distinguished authority on and editor of music of the Baroque and Classical periods, with important writings on Monteverdi, Gluck, and Mozart. Edited many Austrian issues of the *Denkmäler der Tonkunst*.

Hanslick, Eduard (1825–1904). German music critic and civil servant, born in Prague. Studied music with Tomášek and took a doctorate in law at Prague University. His book *Vom Musikalisch Schönen* (1854) was an important contribution to the aesthetics of music. He began to write for the *Neue freie Presse* in Vienna in 1855. He received an honorary readership from the university there in 1856, gave pioneering lectures on music appreciation, and in 1870 became professor of music history and aesthetics.

Hellmesberger, Joseph (1828–93). Austrian conductor, violinist, teacher, wit, and leader of a famous string quartet which bore his name (1849–87). An infant prodigy, he was a member of a family of fine string players which spanned three generations. He was director of the Vienna Conservatory from 1851 till his death, conducted the *Gesellschaft* concerts until 1859, and from 1860 led the orchestra of the Imperial Opera. In 1877 he succeeded Herbeck as chief Kapellmeister to the emperor. His performances of Beethoven's late quartets were among the first to awaken interest in those works. Bruckner taught at the Conservatory under Hellmesberger's direction and Hellmesberger took an erratic interest in his music, commissioning the String Quintet.

Herbeck, Johann (1831–77). Austrian conductor and composer. He succeeded Hellmesberger as conductor of the *Gesellschaftskonzerte* in 1859, became associated with the Vienna Opera in 1863, and its director in 1870. He resigned from the latter post in 1875 owing to continual intrigues. He discovered the original score of Schubert's Unfinished Symphony of which he gave the first performance in 1865. Herbeck was responsible for Bruckner's appointment in Vienna and was one of his most ardent supporters.

Hynais, Cyrill (1867–1914?). Austrian composer and teacher; pupil of Bruckner and editor of some of his works. A faithful disciple, he witnessed Bruckner's last will, acted as his copyist during the last years, and supervised the posthumous publications of Symphony No. 6 and the Andante of the early F minor symphony.

Kalbeck, Max (1850–1921). German music critic, translator of opera librettos, and author of the first full-scale biography of Brahms. He was an unrelenting, hostile critic of Bruckner.

Kattinger, Anton. Organist at St Florian and Bruckner's organ teacher. Bruckner succeeded him in that post in 1848.

Kitzler, Otto (1834–1915). German cellist and conductor, born in Dresden, where he sang in Beethoven's Ninth Symphony under Wagner in 1846. After appointments in Lyon and Königsberg, he became Kapellmeister in Linz, Easter 1861. He was a progressive musician and an early champion of Wagner, conducting the first Linz performance of *Tannhäuser* in 1863. In the same year he left for Temesvár, and in 1865 settled in Brno for the rest of his career as teacher and conductor.

Klose, Friedrich (1862–1942). German composer, pupil of Bruckner. His memoirs contain much of interest regarding his teacher's personality and the Vienna of the 1880s. He wrote a fairy tale opera, *Ilsebill*, 3 symphonic poems, choral works including Masses, and a fine string quartet.

Lachner, Franz (1803–90). Bavarian conductor, prolific composer, pupil of Sechter, and friend of Schubert. His distinguished career as a conductor culminated in his appointment as Hofkapellmeister in Munich (1852). This was terminated prematurely in 1865 because of his antagonism to Wagner. His suites and symphonies achieved great success during his lifetime.

Levi, Hermann (1839–1900). German conductor, originally a friend of Brahms, later on much associated with Wagner whose *Parsifal* he premièred in 1882. In later years he became one of the first leading conductors genuinely interested in Bruckner's music. His notable Mozart interpretations (edition of *Così fan tutte*) anticipated the Mozart revival of this century. He was conductor of the court theatre, Munich, 1872–96.

Löwe, Ferdinand (1865–1925). Austrian conductor, pupil, and disciple of Bruckner. In 1883 he became a piano teacher at the Vienna Conservatory and in 1897 conductor of the Kaim Orchestra, Munich. He edited and published Bruckner's Symphony No. 9 and gave its first performance in 1903. From 1904 to 1924 he was conductor of the Vienna Konzertverein Orchestra, and director of the Vienna Music Academy 1918–22.

Mayfeld, Moritz von (1817–1904). Civil servant and music critic in Linz. Close friend of Bruckner from the time of his appointment as cathedral organist there. Their mutual sympathy and friendship deepened after the première of the D minor Mass (1864) and he was instrumental in encouraging Bruckner to follow the symphonic path. Mayfeld's wife, Betty, was a fine pianist.

Mottl, Felix (1856–1911). Austrian conductor and composer, pupil of Bruckner. Much associated with performances of Wagner at Bayreuth and elsewhere. Conductor at the Karlsruhe opera 1881–1903. Towards the end of a distinguished and successful international career he was appointed director of the opera at Munich (1907).

Nikisch, Arthur (1855–1922). Notable Austro–Hungarian conductor. Child prodigy pianist. Pupil of Hellmesberger and Dessoff. After some years as an orchestral violinist he took up his chosen career, being appointed principal conductor of the Leipzig Opera by 1879. Later he was associated with the Leipzig Gewandhaus Orchestra, the Budapest Opera, the Boston Symphony Orchestra, and the Berlin Philharmonic. He toured widely. An early admirer of Bruckner, he was an outstanding interpreter of the symphonies, and gave the première of No. 7.

Nowak, Leopold (1904–91). Austrian musicologist. He was a pupil of Robert Haas, whom he succeeded in 1945 as director of the music section of the Austrian National Library in Vienna. He was the principal editor of the postwar Complete Edition of Bruckner's works.

Ochs, Siegfried (1858–1929). German choral conductor. He founded the Philharmonic Choir in Berlin and gave early and successful performances of Bruckner's Te Deum, and of choral works by Wolf and Reger. He was sincerely attached to Bruckner in the 1890s.

Pachmann, Vladimir de (1848–1933). Russian pianist of Austrian descent. Pupil of Bruckner. Noted exponent of Chopin with a strongly individualistic and often eccentric style.

Richter, Hans (1943–1916). Austro–Hungarian conductor, studied in Vienna. Worked with Wagner at Tribschen, 1866–7, making a fair score of *Die Meistersinger*. Conducted in Munich 1868–9; in Brussels, 1870; in Budapest 1871–5; in Vienna, 1875. Conducted the first *Ring* cycle, Bayreuth, 1876, and continued to conduct there until 1912. Also a champion of Brahms, giving the premières of his Symphonies 2 and 3. An important early interpreter of Bruckner, giving the premières of his Symphonies 4, 8, and 1 in its Vienna version. From the 1880s much associated with music making in England as opera conductor at Drury Lane and Covent Garden, permanent conductor of the Hallé Orchestra and a prominent champion of Elgar.

Rott, Hans (1858–84). Austrian composer, organist, and favourite pupil of Bruckner. He was appointed organist of the Piaristenkirche, Vienna, in 1877 at which time he was a close friend of Mahler, whose style he strongly anticipated in his Symphony in E. He became insane in 1880.

Rudigier, Franz Josef (1811–84). Bishop of Linz, 1853–84. He was a man of unbending and iron-willed loyalty to the policies of Rome and not afraid to stand up to the Austrian Imperial government against liberal and secular policies. To mark the proclamation of the dogma of the Immaculate Conception of the Virgin Mary he began construction of a new cathedral in Linz and commissioned from Bruckner various works in this connection, including the Mass in E minor. They were close friends: Rudigier was genuinely attached to Bruckner and sent a priest to look after him during his months of nervous breakdown. In turn, Bruckner consoled the bishop in times of conflict and crisis by playing the organ to him alone for many hours. In 1878 he dedicated the motet 'Tota pulchra es Maria' to him.

147

Schalk, Franz (1863–1931). Austrian conductor. He was Bruckner's pupil and most ardent follower, exercising at times great influence on the ageing composer, whose Symphony No. 5 he edited, first performed (1894), and published after Bruckner's death. He was intimately associated with the Vienna Opera for over thirty years, first as Mahler's assistant (in 1900) and finally as artistic director from 1918 (until 1924 in collaboration with Richard Strauss). Also conductor of the *Gesellschaftskonzerte* in Vienna for many years, specializing in the works of Bruckner and Mahler. His memoirs, published posthumously in 1935, contain valuable data on Bruckner's life and work.

Schalk, Joseph (1857–1900). Austrian pianist, writer on music, pupil of Bruckner, and brother of above. His influence on Bruckner was even greater. He advanced the cause of the composer by means of piano arrangements, lectures, programme notes, and pamphlets. He also championed the music of Wolf.

Sechter, Simon (1788–1867). Austrian musical theorist, composer, and teacher. Bruckner was his pupil from 1856–61. Sechter's influence on a man who had been largely self-taught until that time was colossal. For some details of his life and teaching see page 11. One of the most important thinkers about music in the history of that art in Central Europe, he was not only a consummate master of all contrapuntal techniques, but also importantly expanded the harmonic theories of Rameau and Johann Philipp Kirnberger. Following Rameau, he devised the idea of downward diatonic series of fifths and of thirds from which (or from their retrogrades) all chord successions could be explained. From Kirnberger he expanded a theory of 'interpolated roots' which account for all step-by-step movement, up or down, of roots, between which there is a silent fundamental note which has its root a fifth above the second chord.[1] In chromatic music he explained that the harmonies had a diatonic basis; for example, he saw the diminished seventh chord as an incomplete dominant ninth, whose actual root was an unsounded major third below the root of the diminished seventh. His view of chromatic harmony hugely influenced the analyses of Wagner's music by Bruckner's pupils Joseph Schalk and Cyrill Hynais, and the writings of Alfred Lorenz. In its fundamentals, Arnold Schoenberg's *Harmonielehre* was also immensely indebted to Sechter's work.

Seidl, Anton (1850–98). Austro–Hungarian conductor. One of Wagner's assistants at the first Bayreuth Festival, 1876. Appointed conductor of German opera at the New York Metropolitan Opera (1885) and of the New York Philharmonic Society (1891). He gave the first performance of Dvořák's Symphony 'From the New World' in 1893, and the first American performances of several Bruckner symphonies.

Traumihler, Ignaz (1825–84). *Regens Chori* of St Florian from 1852, a Cecilianist and a friend of Bruckner, who dedicated the four-part 'Ave Maria' and the Gradual 'Os justi' to him. In 1877 Bruckner wrote to Traumihler recommending Hans Rott as successor to Josef Seiberl as organist at St Florian.

Weinwurm, Rudolf (1835–1922). Austrian choirmaster and composer. A close friend of Bruckner's, especially during the Linz period, and he helped prepare the way for Bruckner in Vienna. He founded the *Akademische Gesangverein* in Vienna (1858) and was appointed firstly choral instructor (1862) and later musical director (1880) of the university. As an inspector of music he did much to

---

[1] cf. footnote to page 31.

raise the standard of musical education in state-subsidized schools and colleges. His brother Alois was a choral conductor in Linz.

Weiss, Johann Baptist (1813–50). Composer, organist, and teacher at Hörsching, near Linz. He was a first cousin to Bruckner, his mother being a sister of Bruckner's father. In 1833 he became Bruckner's godfather and was his teacher throughout 1835 and 1836. His Masses and other small liturgical works were important models for Bruckner during his early years of composition. He committed suicide.

Witt, Franz Xaver (1834–88). German priest and composer of sacred music. In 1867 he founded the *Caecilienverein*, the aim of which was the improvement of Roman Catholic church music through the restoration of a Palestrinian a cappella style and the total exclusion of the orchestra from devotional music. He edited the periodical *Musica Sacra*, which published in 1885 Bruckner's 'Pange lingua et Tantum ergo' of 1868.

Wöss, Josef Venantius von (1863–1943). Austrian composer and music teacher. He edited, published, and made piano arrangements of many works by Bruckner. He knew Bruckner and wrote a memoir of him.

Zenetti, Leopold von (1805–92). Organist, composer, and music teacher at Enns, Upper Austria. He taught Bruckner from 1843 to 1845.

Appendix D

Select bibliography

The following list makes no attempt to include all the literature on Bruckner, and refers only to books and articles that may broaden the scope for the general reader of this volume. Of the studies in English, the books of Doernberg and Schönzeler contain admirable biographies, whilst Simpson's *The Essence of Bruckner* is the most readable and penetrating analytical approach to the symphonies for the reader who has some knowledge of score-reading and harmony. Among the more scholarly writings in German, the books by Auer, Haas, Nowak, and Orel are strongly recommended. The four-volume study by Göllerich and Auer is the standard work on Bruckner: it contains a wealth of detailed information not found elsewhere. The publications of the Anton Bruckner-Institut Linz have added more than any to the literature in terms of biography, documentation, interpretation, and editorial aspects since 1979. Their imprint is the Musikwissenschaftlicher Verlag, Vienna, and I have listed their volumes at the end.

Abendroth, Walter, *Die Symphonien Anton Bruckners* (Leipzig, 1940).
Auer, Max, *Anton Bruckner, sein Leben und Werk*, 6th edn. (Vienna, 1966).
Blume, F., 'Bruckner' in *Die Musik in Geschichte und Gegenwart*, vol. 2 (Cassel, 1952).
Bruckner, Anton, *Gesammelte Briefe,* ed. Gräflinger and Auer, 2 vols. (Regensburg, 1924).
—— *Vorlesungen über Harmonielehre und Kontrapunkt*, ed. E. Schwanzara (Vienna, 1951).
—— *Briefe*, ed. Otto Schneider and Andrea Harrandt, 2 vols., to form vol. xxiv of the *Anton Bruckner Kritische Gesamtausgabe* (Vienna, in preparation).
Brunner, Franz, *Dr Anton Bruckner* (Linz, 1895).
Chord and Discord, 'Journal of the Bruckner Society of America' (1932 fol.).
Cooke, Deryck, 'The Bruckner Problem simplified', *The Musical Times*, 110, Jan., Feb., May, and Aug. 1969; reprinted in Cooke, *Vindications: Essays on Romantic Music* (London, 1982).
—— Article 'Bruckner' in *The New Grove* (London, 1980).
Dawson-Bowling, Paul, 'Thematic and tonal unity in Bruckner's Eighth Symphony', *The Music Review*, August 1969.
Decsey, Ernst, *Bruckner: Versuch eines Lebens* (Berlin, 1919).
Dehnert, Max, *Anton Bruckner, Versuch einer Deutung* (Leipzig, 1958).
Doernberg, Erwin, *The life and symphonies of Anton Bruckner* (London, 1960).
Eckstein, Friedrich, *Erinnerungen an Anton Bruckner* (Vienna, 1923).

Engel, Gabriel, *The Symphonies of Anton Bruckner* (New York, 1955).

Fischer, Hans Conrad, *Anton Bruckner—Sein Leben* (Salzburg, 1974).

Gallois, Jean, *Bruckner* (Paris, 1971).

Gilliam, Bryan, 'The Two Versions of Bruckner's Eighth Symphony', *19th-Century Music*, 16/1, 1992, pp. 59–69.

Göllerich, August and Auer, Max, *Anton Bruckner*, 4 vols. in 9 (Regensburg, 1922–36; reprinted 1974).

Gräflinger, Franz, *Anton Bruckner: Leben und Schaffen* (Vienna, 1948).

—— *Liebes und Heiteres um Anton Bruckner* (Vienna, 1948).

Grüninger, Fritz, *Anton Bruckner: der metaphysische Kern seiner Persönlichkeit und Werke* (Augsburg, 1930).

—— *Der Ehrfürchtige: Anton Bruckners Leben dem Volke erzählt* (Freiburg i.B., 1937).

—— *Der Meister von Sankt Florian—Wege zu Anton Bruckner* (Augsburg, 1950).

Haas, Robert, *Anton Bruckner* (Potsdam, 1934).

Halm, August, *Die Symphonie Anton Bruckners* (Munich, 1914).

Hawkshaw, Paul, 'The Date of Bruckner's "Nullified" Symphony in D minor', *19th-Century Music*, 6, 1982, pp. 252–63.

Howie, A. C., 'Traditional and Novel Elements in Bruckner's Sacred Music', *Musical Quarterly*, lxvii/4, pp. 544–67.

Hruby, C., *Meine Erinnerungen an Anton Bruckner* (Vienna, 1901).

Jackson, Timothy L., 'Bruckner's Metrical Numbers', *19th-Century Music*, 12, 1990, pp. 101–31.

Johnson, Stephen, *Bruckner Remembered* (London, 1996).

Kitzler, Otto, *Musikalische Erinnerungen* (Brno, 1904).

Klose, Friedrich, *Meine Lehrjahre bei Bruckner* (Regensburg, 1927).

Krohn, Ilmari, *Anton Bruckners Symphonien: Untersuchung über Formenbau und Stimmungsgehalt*, 3 vols. (Helsinki, 1955–7).

Kurth, Ernst, *Bruckner*, 2 vols. (Berlin, 1925).

Langevin, Paul-Gilbert, *Le Siècle de Bruckner* (Paris, 1975) [Special number of *La Revue Musicale* 298/299].

Lassl, Josef, *Das kleine Brucknerbuch* (Salzburg, 1965).

Leibnitz, Thomas, *Die Brüder Schalk und Anton Bruckner* (Tutzing, 1988).

Linninger, F., *Orgeln und Organisten im Stift St Florian* (Linz, 1955).

Machabey, Armand, *La Vie et l'œuvre d'Anton Bruckner* (Paris, 1945).

Mahling, Christoph-Hellmut, *Anton Bruckner: Studien zu Werke und Wirkung* (Tutzing, 1988).

Newlin, Dika, *Bruckner–Mahler–Schoenberg* (New York, 1947).

Nowak, Leopold, *Anton Bruckner, Musik und Leben* (Linz, 1973).

—— *Über Anton Bruckner: Gesammelte Aufsätze 1936–1984* (Vienna, 1985).

Oberleitner, Max von, *Meine Erinnerungen an Anton Bruckner* (Regensburg, 1933).

Oeser, Fritz, *Die Klangstruktur der Bruckner-Symphonie* (Leipzig, 1939).

Orel, Alfred, *Anton Bruckner, das Werk, der Künstler, die Zeit* (Vienna, 1925).

—— *Anton Bruckner, sein Leben in Bildern* (Vienna, 1936).

—— *Bruckner Brevier* (Vienna, 1953).

Parkany, Stephen, 'Kurth's *Bruckner* and the Adagio of the Seventh Symphony', *19th-Century Music*, 11/3, 1988, pp. 262–81.

Raynor, H., 'An Approach to Anton Bruckner', *The Musical Times*, 96, Feb. 1955.

Redlich, Hans Ferdinand, *Bruckner and Mahler* (London, 1955).
Reich, Willi, *Anton Bruckner—ein Bild seiner Persönlichkeit* (Basel, 1953).
Schalk, Franz, *Briefe und Betrachtungen* (Vienna, 1935).
Schönzeler, Hans-Hubert, *Bruckner* (London, 1970; rev. 1978).
Schwanzara, Ernst, *Anton Bruckners Stamm und Urheimat* (Regensburg, 1937).
—— (ed.), *Bruckner: Vorlesen über Harmonielehre und Kontrapunkt an der Universität Wien* (Vienna, 1953).
Simpson, Robert, *Bruckner and the symphony* (London, 1963).
—— *The Essence of Bruckner* (London 1967; rev. 1992).
Tschulik, Norbert, *Anton Bruckner im Spiegel seiner Zeit* (Vienna, 1965).
Vassenhove, Leon van, *Anton Bruckner* (Neuchâtel, 1942).
Wagner, Manfred, *Bruckner* (Mainz, 1983).
Wehle, Gerhard F., *Anton Bruckner im Spiegel seiner Zeitgenossen* (Garmisch-Partenkirchen, 1964).
Wessely, Othmar, *Bruckner-Studien 1824–1974* (Vienna, 1975).
Wetz, Richard, *Anton Bruckner, sein Leben und Schaffen* (Leipzig, 1922).
Wolff, Werner, *Anton Bruckner: Rustic Genius* (New York, 1942).
Wöss, Kurt, *Ratschläge zur Aufführung der Sinfonien Anton Bruckners* (Linz, 1974).

Publications of the Anton Bruckner-Institut, Linz

(A) DOKUMENTE UND STUDIEN
  (1) Antonicek, Theophil, *Anton Bruckner und die Wiener Hofmusikkapelle*, ed. Franz Grasberger, 1979
  (2) Grasberger, Franz (ed.), *Anton Bruckner in Wien*, 1980
  (3) Grasberger, Franz (ed.), *Anton Bruckner und Leopold von Zenetti*, 1980
  (4) Grasberger, Renate, *Bruckner-Bibliographie (bis 1964)*, 1985
  (5) Kreczi, Hanns, *Das Bruckner-Stift St Florian und das Linzer Reichs-Bruckner-Orchester 1942–1945*, 1986
  (6) Lieberwirth, Steffen, *Anton Bruckner und Leipzig*, 1988
  (7) Grasberger, Renate, *Bruckner-Ikonographie*, 1990
  (8) Grasberger, R. and Partsch, Erich Wolfgang, *Bruckner-Skizziert*, 1991
  (9) Kreczi, Hanns, *Bruckner-Orchester und Brucknerhaus Linz*, 1992
 (10) Wessely, O. (ed.), *Staat-Kirche-Schule in Oberösterreich*, 1994

(B) BRUCKNER-JAHRBÜCHER: seven volumes have appeared for 1980/1981/1982–3/1984–5–6/1987–8/1989–90/1991–2–3

(C) BRUCKNER-SYMPOSIUMSBERICHTE
  (1) *Die Fassungen*, ed. F. Grasberger, 1991
  (2) *Die Österreichische Symphonie nach Anton Bruckner*, ed. O. Wessely, 1983
  (3) *Bruckner-Interpretation*, ed. O. Wessely, 1983
  (4) *Johannes Brahms und Anton Bruckner*, ed. O. Wessely, 1985
  (5) *Bruckner, Wagner und die Neudeutschen in Österreich*, ed. O. Wessely, 1986
  (6) *Anton Bruckner und die Kirchenmusik*, ed. O. Wessely, 1988
  (7) *Bruckner, Liszt, Mahler und die Moderne*, R. Grasberger et al., 1989
  (8) *Bruckner und die Musik der Romantik*, R. Grasberger et al., 1989
  (9) *Anton Bruckner als Schüler und Lehrer*, ed. O. Wessely et al., 1992
 (10) *Orchestermusik im 19. Jahrhundert*, ed. O. Wessely et al., 1992
 (11) *Musikstadt Linz—Musikland Oberösterreich*, ed. O. Wessely et al., 1993

(12) *Bruckner-Rezeption*, ed. O. Wessely et al., 1994
(13) *Persönlichkeit und Werk*, ed. O. Wessely et al., 1995
(14) *Entwicklungen-Parallelen-Kontraste*, ed. O. Wessely et al., 1995

(D) BRUCKNER VORTRÄGE

(1) Bruckner-Vorträge Budapest 1983/4, ed. O. Wessely, 1985
(2) Bruckner-Vorträge Rom 1986 (A. Bruckner e la musica sacra), ed. O. Wessely, 1987

Index

Index

Index